THE MOTHER OF ALL

OPPORTUNITIES

A strategy for a decade of growth,
profits and market share gains

Katrina McCarter

'Most companies, whether start-ups or not, arrogantly assume from their own collective experiences what their customer wants and how to sell to them. In some cases this may be more than just a contributing factor in failure. We employed Katrina and found her absolutely insightful and invaluable. These insights will mean we don't disenfranchise our customers, and will save us time and funds. We were so impressed by Katrina, we offered her a role on our board. I would recommend Katrina to anyone targeting mums.'
Ken Matthews, Chairperson, KidNest

'*The Mother of All Opportunities* is a fascinating insight into "the most influential consumer segment in the world", and required reading for any CEO, CMO or Sales Leader who counts mums as part of their target audience. In her first book, Katrina McCarter focused on how to reach and better serve Australian mums. In this second book, Katrina takes a more global perspective, sharing stories about the best (and worst) behaviours of businesses that market to mums and exploring the trends shaping this critical market segment. This book delivers a step-by-step guide to creating strong, lasting and mutually beneficial relationships with mums all over the world, in a way that's authentic, empathetic and fun.'
Cian Mcloughlin, Amazon Bestselling Author,
Keynote Speaker & Sales Expert

'Katrina McCarter is without doubt a global leader when it comes to the extraordinary opportunity that is the "mum" market. She has an incredible depth of knowledge and experience, backed up with detailed research. Corporations around the world need to listen to what Katrina has to say.'
Andrew Griffiths, International Bestselling Author and Global Speaker

'Katrina McCarter is Australia's number one expert in marketing to mums, and an unrivalled thought leader in this space. In *The Mother of All Opportunities*, she shares her expertise and years of experience to help businesses capitalise on this massive – and growing – opportunity. She also includes research and insights from other leading global experts, and identifies the key trends for the coming decade. Businesses, big and small, cannot afford to continue to ignore or undervalue this lucrative global market segment. I highly recommend this book.'

Kate Christie, CEO Time Stylers

'Katrina's speaking style is a unique combination of sparkling and straightforward (in the best possible way!). She always leaves her audience with insightful implications that both delight and satisfy! She is truly an expert on "mums" and brings an excellent perspective to the kid and family space as both a captivating presenter and a thoughtful client advisor. Katrina is an excellent collaborator and supportive colleague, always looking to bring the best thinking to the world through smart partnerships.'

Amy Henry, President, FlashLight Insights

'Katrina was an expert speaker at our recent event Engaging Mums with your Brand in Australia and China. Hosting 70 influential brand owners, Katrina had the audience captivated with her amazing data-driven insights about the most important customer for brands – mums. Katrina provides brands with actionable strategies all can implement to gain the trust of mums. We can't wait to engage Katrina again for projects and future events with Tell Me Baby. I can highly recommend working with Katrina.'

Mat Colbron, CEO, Tell Me Group

ACKNOWLEDGEMENTS

I'd like to thank the following people for their contributions to the book and, in many cases, for their ongoing support in my work at Marketing to Mums:

Mita Mallick, Unilever North America

Phillip Lynch, Johnson & Johnson Asia Pacific

Bill Partyka, Gerber Products Company

Mike Johnstone, Volvo Cars UK

Wendy Liebmann, WSL Strategic Retail

Kate Torgersen, Milk Stork

Jola Burnett, GfK

Michelle Poris, Smarty Pants

Anoushka Gungadin, Global CQ

Patty David, AARP

Nan McCann, M2Moms® – the Marketing to Moms conference

Catherine Cervasio, Aromababy

Wendy Olson Killion, Expedia Group Media Solutions

Roshni Mahtani, Tickled Media

Larissa Vince, Saatchi & Saatchi London

Dannielle Michaels, b.box for kids

Amy Henry, FlashLight Insights

Marija Butkovic, Women of Wearables

Christine Michel Carter, Minority Woman Marketing

David Butler, Be Curious Partners

Stacey Hicks, *Girlfriend*, Pacific Magazines

Liz O'Donnell, WorkingDaughter.com

Dino Jaegle, WeMoms France

Simone Lindus, Tiny Tutus

Melissa DeCesare, Edison Research
Jeff Fromm, Futurecast
Sarah Bartholomeusz, You Legal
Hansa Bhargava, WebMD
Andrew Griffiths, Andrew Griffiths Enterprises
Alice Dupuche, A Woman To Watch
David Willey, Growth Tank
Kath Blackham, VERSA
Bridget Brennan, The Female Factor
Michael Hanrahan, Publish Central
Bec Brideson, Women With Agency
Skyler Mattson, WONGDOODY
Emma Lovell, CoziGo
Kristy Chong, Modibodi
Jennifer Holland, ThroatScope
Carrie Kwan, Mums & Co
Stevie Angel and Nadia Tucker, Active Truth
Chris Tistrand, Dinner Twist
Roslyn Johnson, Aquacove
Andrea Scalzo Yi, Raising Dragons
Loren Bartley, Impactiv8
Kelly Glover, The Talent Squad
Cinzia Cozzolino, Smoothie Bombs
Sam Jockel, Parent TV
Sean Callanan, Sports Geek

And to the thousands of mothers who participate in the Marketing to Mums ongoing research.

ABOUT KATRINA McCARTER

Katrina McCarter is the founder and CEO of Marketing to Mums, a marketing and research consultancy based in Melbourne, Australia. She is a Marketing Strategist, Bestselling Author, International Award-winning Speaker and Business Advisor. Katrina specialises in helping businesses sell more effectively to mums, the world's most powerful consumer, and provides strategic, research and educational support to brands in Australia and overseas.

In 2016 Katrina published her first book *Marketing to Mums: How to sell more to Australia's most powerful consumer*. It was written for small business owners to provide them with an eight-step framework to improve their sales among mothers. Her book quickly went to number one on Booktopia's Business Bestseller List, outselling the likes of Simon Sinek, Timothy Ferriss and Sophia Amoruso. It is now in its fifth reprint and sells copies across the world.

Katrina is a data-driven marketer who regularly engages in research to deeply understand mothers across the world. She shares her findings speaking at conferences and brand events throughout Australia and overseas. In October 2018 she won the 'You Take the Cake' Best Speaker Award in New York after delivering the closing keynote address at M2Moms® – the Marketing to Moms conference. In September 2018 she was the only English-speaking presenter invited to speak in Paris and share her research at the Moms & Marketing conference.

In late 2018 Katrina launched the world's first podcast covering marketing to mums, where she interviews brand leaders, researchers and marketing specialists to better understand mums' changing behaviours and help brands drive their sales and profit. The podcast debuted at number six on Apple Podcasts in the Business section and has a growing following.

Katrina is a sought-after media commentator and has featured in TV, radio, print and digital media. In 2017, 2018 and 2019 she was named a finalist in B&T's Women in Media awards in Australia (Entrepreneur and Marketing categories).

How to contact Katrina

For speaking enquires:

www.katrinamccarter.com

katrina@katrinamccarter.com

For consulting and advisory engagements:

www.marketingtomums.com.au

katrina@marketingtomums.com.au

For media enquiries:

www.katrinamccarter.com/media

katrina@marketingtomums.com.au

CONTENTS

INTRODUCTION

A massive market that most brands are missing out on

Did you know that mothers worldwide are responsible for spending more than the combined global brand valuations of the world's top 100 brands?[1]

Did you know that American mothers control spending that is considerably larger than the 2019 global brand valuations of Amazon, Apple, Google, Microsoft, Visa, Facebook, Alibaba, Tencent, McDonald's and AT&T combined – every single year?[2]

Did you know that American mothers control spending higher than the GDP of Italy, the world's eighth-largest economy?[3]

Did you know that if Australian mothers were an industry they would be the largest contributor to GDP?[4]

Did you know that mothers control spending for more than 130 million babies born each year?

1 www.millwardbrown.com/global-navigation/news/press-releases/full-release/2019/06/11/accelerated-growth-sees-amazon-crowned-2019-s-brandztm-top-100-most-valuable-global-brand

2 www.millwardbrown.com/global-navigation/news/press-releases/full-release/2019/06/11/accelerated-growth-sees-amazon-crowned-2019-s-brandztm-top-100-most-valuable-global-brand

3 www.focus-economics.com/blog/the-largest-economies-in-the-world

4 https://campaignbrief.com/reborn-lion-co-uncover-how-bra/

Did you know that Australian mothers are responsible for spending almost double the annual sales revenue of Alibaba, China's most valuable brand?[1]

These are staggering numbers, and they demonstrate why mothers are the powerhouse of the global economy, responsible for more than 80% of spending every single year. Their economic power is indisputable. And it is growing.

Why mothers are the most compelling market on the planet

Women change the way they shop and interact with brands once they become mothers. They adopt a new role: Chief Buyer and Influencer. But many brands miss this change. In their roles as mothers, women buy for multiple people and also influence the buying decisions of all those around them. When women become mothers they are eight times more likely to talk about brands,[2] so building and capitalising on meaningful relationships with mothers is critical to most brands to fuel customer advocacy as consumers increasingly reject corporate sales messages.

Mothers' breadth of spending has grown significantly over the past decade. These highly educated women are now starting their own businesses in record numbers across the world. In Australia, women are entering business at almost three times the rate of men, and have been for more than 10 years. They are seeking meaningful work and more flexible work arrangements after the birth of a child. These working mothers are influencing categories from legal, accounting and advertising services through to travel and healthcare. As their entrepreneurial endeavours mature their influence expands, as do the opportunities for brands.

---

1 www.millwardbrown.com/global-navigation/news/press-releases/full-release/2019/06/11/accelerated-growth-sees-amazon-crowned-2019-s-brandztm-top-100-most-valuable-global-brand

2 fleishmanhillard.com/2019/05/brand-marketing/marketing-to-mom-at-mothers-day/

Across the world mothers are demanding that brands earn their attention and respect. As early adopters of technology, mothers have also become highly sophisticated shoppers. They are an exceptionally well researched consumer group. Not only can they filter content rapidly, they have developed shortcuts to find the information they need quickly and from a trusted source: other mothers. Their expectations of brands are high. Any mother who approaches a retailer has done her homework. Now, more than ever, brands need to invest heavily in building relationships with mothers in the early stages of their customer journey.

A mum expert and advisor

I've been studying mums for two decades. I have 18 years' sales and marketing experience working across diverse industries, including consumer goods, healthcare, automotive, hardware, ecommerce and more, always targeting mothers in their role of chief household buyer. I also have a Bachelor of Business (Marketing) and an MBA (International Business). However, my real learning happened when I became a mother myself. I left my corporate role to enjoy a five-year career break to raise my three children. As a stay-at-home mum, I spent hours in the park listening to the frustrations and challenges facing mothers.

Eight years ago, I launched an online shopping platform for mums which I grew to a community of 150,000 before selling it in 2016. During this time, my insight into mums really accelerated and I gained a deeper understanding of mums' lives. I learned how to engage mums and build a community, communicate effectively with them through social media, and convert them to a sale. It provided fertile ground to understand the buying behaviours of mothers, what attracted them to brands and what repelled them.

Working closely with brands, I also saw the struggles they had in managing to genuinely connect with and sell to mums. I kept seeing the same problems over and over: businesses needed new

3

customers, but didn't have the expertise or the strategy to sell to mums, which meant they were missing out on a very lucrative market segment. Their poor ROI proved that they didn't have a clear understanding of the type of mum they were wanting to attract. They needed my help.

There exists a growing wave of dissatisfaction with brands among mothers. Mums across the globe feel misunderstood, misrepresented and undervalued. They feel there is a lack of progress in delivering against their expectations. Ignoring this growing dissatisfaction is commercially disastrous for brands. Astute marketers, however, who take the time to gather deep insights about mums and work to earn their attention can deliver a significant commercial advantage in an increasingly crowded marketplace.

This combination of personal experience and seeing the problems businesses were facing led me to create Marketing to Mums in 2015, my marketing and research consultancy where I provide strategic, research and educational support to brands. I work with companies and boards as their resident mum expert and advisor, using my expertise and comprehensive research data to guide and improve their plans. I educate boards and senior teams, facilitate strategy workshops, build and review marketing strategies, and speak at conferences across the world to share my research and insights.

Despite the growing economic power and influence of mothers, many brands have never felt more challenging conditions, and growth feels under threat. Global population growth rates have halved since the 1960s, with the 2018–19 projected population growth rate falling to 1.07%. No longer can brands simply rely on population increases to fuel their growth strategy. I've also repeatedly witnessed brands struggling to keep up with the rapidly changing behaviours of mothers in their market. With so many tools and tactics now available, they've been increasingly challenged to understand how best to increase sales conversions among this lucrative consumer group.

I've written this book to help board directors, C-suite executives and senior management teams across the globe who are searching for where they might find their future growth. I want to help unlock growth for you in your business. I've gone out to brand leaders, leading market researchers, agency chiefs and marketing specialists and asked them to share their insights and ideas about where they see opportunity over the next decade. You'll hear views from senior executives working at J&J, Unilever, GfK, WSL Strategic Retail, Saatchi & Saatchi and Volvo, among others. And I have of course included my own thoughts, experience and research. Together, we guide you through a series of opportunities that can act as a starting point for further investigation to help your business find its way in with this often misunderstood market.

The next decade

Fast forward to 2030. What will mums respond to? I've consulted brand leaders and senior marketers from a range of industries and I've predicted eight key success strategies your brand needs to consider over the coming decade. It will help you identify your capability requirements and allow you to embrace new ways that mothers are interacting.

This book represents an opportunity for you to rethink your brand's strategy for and relationship with the largest, most influential consumer segment in the world. I ask you to bring an open mind and leave your old ways of thinking at the door. As you'll read in these pages, many companies have made mistakes trying to connect with this lucrative market, and that may include yours.

Successful brands in the mum market will understand the importance of research and data. They will adopt a more collaborative approach, throw out the current rulebook, and recognise that mothers are their best ally for future growth. They will be committed to a long game. And more than anything, they will be willing to invest the time and resources required into this lucrative, influential and largely untapped consumer market. I will show you the many opportunities that exist, and can assist you to get an edge over your competitors and gain growth. You can pick up this book and read it chapter by chapter, or pick an opportunity in any order.

There are new ways to communicate with and sell to mums, delivering massive opportunities for businesses that get it right. The potential to find growth, profits and market share among mothers over the next decade is simply extraordinary.

This is the mother of all opportunities.

The choice and the opportunity are yours.

Katrina McCarter

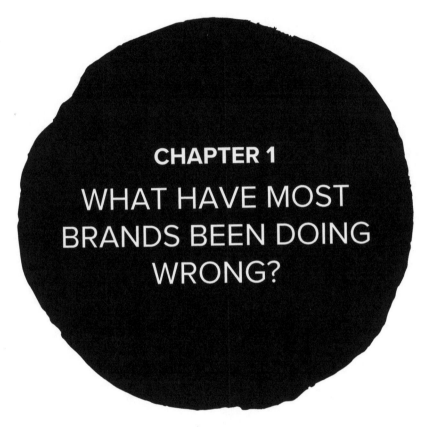

CHAPTER 1

WHAT HAVE MOST BRANDS BEEN DOING WRONG?

In all sorts of research over many years, mothers have repeatedly made it very clear they are unhappy with the way brands are communicating with them. It's been 10 years since it was reported that 91% of women feel advertisers don't understand them.[1] And three years ago, our research at Marketing to Mums found that 63% of Australian mothers felt brands and advertisers don't understand them. So, little has changed over the years – and there lies the huge opportunity for your brand right now. If you can avoid the common mistakes that so many brands make when trying to reach mums, you'll be able to separate yourself from your competitors and start to make inroads into this often misunderstood market.

At Marketing to Mums we have found that mothers in Australia feel very strongly that advertisers fail to engage them appropriately. And the level of dissatisfaction varies significantly based on the age of the mother, with Generation X being the most dissatisfied with brand communications.

Despite being such a lucrative market, they remain unhappy with the way they are being communicated with. So, what mistakes are brands making over and over again? I've been researching where brands are going wrong for many years, undertaking extensive quantitative and qualitative research. I have identified seven key mistakes being made by companies trying to reach this highly profitable market:

1. They target too broadly.

2. They think they know the mum market – and they are wrong.

3. They don't invest in mum research.

4. They don't seek out C-suite and board support.

5. They fail to stay connected with the customer.

6. They rely too heavily on their advertising agency.

7. They don't involve mums in their new product development.

---

1   m2w.biz/fast-facts/

Let's have a look at each of these.

Mistake #1: They target too broadly

Perhaps the greatest mistake I see is brands targeting too broadly, and they treat mothers as one homogenous group. In a 2019 Marketing to Mums study of 656 Australian mums, 55% of them felt that brands treat mums like they are all the same. As the chief shopper in most families, mothers have become far more sophisticated, and they expect more tailored offerings. Different segments of the market require a different approach and have different communication preferences. Businesses that are prepared to micro-niche and introduce a greater level of segmentation are yielding superior results. They are gaining a competitive advantage. Why? Because they are laser-focused on who they are communicating with. They understand their 'core mum' at a much deeper level than their competitors.

> 'Advertisers need to recognise that not all mums are one homogeneous group. We don't suddenly lose our identity once we have children, but it does change. They have to take the time to understand the market segments that exist under the "mum" umbrella and tailor their products and services accordingly.'
>
> *Marketing to Mums Survey (2019)*

Micro-niching also results in a reduction of marketing wastage, as the selection of channels and tactics implemented better matches their most profitable core mother segment. Consequently, return on investment (ROI) increases.

The correct identification of your most profitable segment of the mum market is a critical factor in your success. It remains a foundation that I frequently see brands overlook.

I spoke with Roshni Mahtani, founder of theAsianparent which reaches over 23 million women monthly across Southeast Asia.

It's available in nine languages in 12 countries (Singapore, Malaysia, Thailand, Indonesia, Philippines, Vietnam, India, Sri Lanka, Hong Kong, Taiwan, Nigeria and Japan). Their app has over 1.5 million downloads, and is the number one parenting app in Southeast Asia.

I wanted to understand what Roshni felt was the biggest mistake brands made when entering the Asian market:

'Lumping Asian mums as one category and employing a "one size fits all" strategy is the biggest mistake. There is a huge difference between a Thai mum versus an Indonesian mum versus a Malaysian mum. For example, Singaporean mums are more dependent on daycare, whereas Filipino mums have nannies and maids. Indian mums rely on Ayurvedic healing and remedies. Chinese mums across the region practice postpartum "confinement" – Taiwan even has a luxury industry built around it. Indonesian, Thai, Japanese, Sri Lankan and Vietnamese audiences favour content in their respective local languages. Buddhism, Catholicism, Hinduism and Islam aren't even all of the religions practised in Asia. New Year celebrations aren't just on 1 January.

'So, no industry is spared by this fragmentation. The differences across cultures have an impact on decisions made by the family when it comes to their health and nutrition, education, finance, travel, fashion, media and other matters of lifestyle.

'Marketers do their brands a great disservice when they stereotype or think that their existing product will fit neighbouring countries as seamlessly as in the launch market.'

Mistake #2: They think they know the mum market – and they are wrong

There exists an attitude of 'we know mums' among many marketing teams and senior managements. In my work with different brands

I see this often. But these brands fail to acknowledge how quickly mums' behaviours are changing. They don't realise their thinking is outdated, and – without realising – they start relying on stereotyping. In our recent Marketing to Mums research, Australian mothers identified that stereotyping about mums was the number one mistake brands make. In many instances this is driven by senior management holding unconscious biases about who mothers are, based on their own experiences with raising children 20 or 30 years ago. It's a view shared by Jola Burnett, Vice President at GfK:

'The biggest mistake brands make when marketing to moms is inadvertently engaging in hidden gender bias or downright stereotyping. Today's moms are more educated than their mothers and grandmothers ever were. They are taking on new roles, pushing the boundaries and making more decisions than ever before. There is also a significant evolution taking place, impacting household dynamics and establishing new roles and responsibilities. Some marketers make the mistake of portraying unattainable and unrealistic versions of moms, which can fuel stress and disappointment.'

It's essential that board members remain well informed about trends and key changes within the mum market, and hold their senior marketers accountable by bringing in a mum specialist who can share the latest research. Such specialists also bring with them the latest thinking and learnings about what's working in other industries. Mums are changing rapidly, and brands must stay informed and connected to their customers to stay relevant and to capitalise on this opportunity.

'Try to interact with me and get to know a little bit more about me first before you advertise all this nonsense that is not even relevant to me. You can also stop pigeonholing mothers and making it seem like we're all the same. We are unique

individual women, and treating mothers like they are idiotic and incompetent at making their own decisions is not right.'

Marketing to Mums survey (2019)

Mistake #3: They don't invest in mum research

In recent years I've noticed some resistance to undertaking regular market research by brands. They cite pressure on their budget and tight timeframes issued from senior management. They launch new products and services into the market based on assumptions and previous learnings, and to 'just get on with things'. This approach makes my head ache. It's shortsighted and dangerous for the business. Staying relevant by staying connected with your core mum customer is one of the most important factors in a brand's success in this market. Once relevance is lost it's unlikely to return as mothers have very long memories. Regular research, both formal and informal, is something which should be high on the list of priorities.

I worked with a global brand who were wanting to drive their ecommerce sales in their home country. They were adamant they knew exactly who their customer was, however my ongoing research into mothers told me otherwise. After weeks of discussion they agreed to allow me to run market research to identify the most profitable segment of the mum market for them. To their surprise, their most profitable segment was the *opposite* of what they thought it was. Rather than a young mother in her mid-20s who was highly aspirational and 'on trend', our Marketing to Mums research revealed she was actually a mother aged 45 years who was repelled by aspirational efforts to reach her. The research findings led me to create a new marketing strategy to attract more mothers aged over 45 years. After eight months it had yielded more than a 500% increase in their online sales compared with the same time period the previous year.

I always recommend that even if you think you know your market, invest in a research project to identify the most profitable niche for your brand. It's likely to provide a significant ROI as your marketing team will then be able to select more tailored and better suited channels, influencers and tactics. I strongly believe you need accurate, up-to-date data points to underpin and guide your mum marketing strategy.

Don't pretend you know what mums want. Do your research and ask.

Mistake #4: They don't seek out C-suite and board support

Successful brands are led by visionary brand leaders who are supported by a productive board. Where I see issues is when senior marketers haven't built a strong enough case for their marketing strategy. They fail to effectively share their vision highlighting the opportunity within the mum market. As a result, they don't get the budget support for the foundation work they wish to undertake to build a robust mum strategy to position the brand for long-term success. Instead, they engage in short-term sales strategies based on limited knowledge (as there's no budget for research). Over time brand equity is eroded, loyalty diminishes and a significant financial opportunity is missed.

Progressive boards and C-suite executives recognise the value of the mum market and its importance to the brand's success. They keep themselves up to date with relevant market shifts by engaging with specialist advisors. Most importantly, they take a long-term view and ensure they have built strong brand foundations first. Increasingly, I'm asked to brief boards, senior management and marketing teams to ensure they are abreast of new trends and have awareness around behavioural changes.

Mistake #5: They fail to stay connected with the customer

As people move up in an organisation, without realising it they become stuck in their ivory tower. They enter an echo chamber where they rely only on their teams to deliver information about consumer changes, marketing techniques and relevant strategies. In doing so, they lose touch with their customer: mums. This will cause the brand to:

- quickly lose relevance
- diminish customer loyalty
- lose market share
- have trust issues with customers
- miss significant opportunities.

Once relevance is lost, these brands experience a very long, slow climb back. Mums don't forget quickly.

Brands are missing the mark by portraying mothers as beautiful, confident and fit, and failing to understand how busy, emotional and anxious they feel, thereby repelling the very audience they wish to attract. A Canadian study undertaken by BabyCenter found only 15% of mothers feel that brands realistically portray them.[1]

Kate Torgersen, founder of Milk Stork – the first breast milk shipping service for business travelling, breastfeeding mothers – sums it well, saying:

> *'I see a lot of marketing that simplifies the mom experience to quiet, cuddly moments. In reality, being a mom is an adventure that requires immense amounts of grit, physical and emotional endurance, and smarts. It's a big "miss" when marketing fails to acknowledge the strength and acumen that it takes to be a mom.'*

---

1 marketingmag.ca/consumer/the-problem-with-marketing-to-moms-survey-173692/

Mistake #6: They rely too heavily on their advertising agency

According to a PwC study, the average profile of someone working in an advertising agency in Australia is a 27-year-old white male with no children.[1] They will have trouble empathising with mothers. But these young, male agency executives are being relied on to come up with ideas and creative content to connect with mothers. It results in campaigns that really miss the point, with marketing funds being wasted and brand credibility put at great risk.

It's a similar story the world over; advertising agencies aren't conducive to motherhood, with late hours often required, forcing many mothers to look for more family-friendly industries to work in. It's having an impact on the quality of work being produced for the mum market.

Independent research, ensuring you have mums on all your external teams, and keeping control of your strategy are critical to success.

It's a belief shared by my US colleague Skyler Mattson. Skyler is the President of WONGDOODY, an Ad Age Agency of the Year, whom I've had the pleasure of knowing after speaking at the same event for the past two years. She says:

'One of the most critical things you can do as a marketer who targets mothers is ensure there are mothers on your external agency teams. They will bring an authentic perspective to your communications and also make sure you avoid embarrassing (and often costly) mistakes. Recently a car manufacturer produced a television commercial showing a small infant in a front-facing car seat. The day after it aired the mothers at our agency were appalled – of course they should know you don't place infants facing the front. One of my colleagues exclaimed, "clearly there were no moms on that team".'

---

1 www.adnews.com.au/news/age-is-the-new-diversity-problem-in-advertising

Mistake #7: They don't involve mums in their new product development

Many brands have a core group of highly engaged customers who consistently advocate for their brand. This represents an opportunity to seek feedback and get your target customers involved in creating new products. In our Marketing to Mums research, mums have strongly voiced that they want to be actively involved in product and service development for the brands they love. It makes them feel appreciated, they'll get better products, and they can guide the brand to greater success. Everybody wins.

I discussed this with Bridget Brennan, CEO of US-based Female Factor Corporation and author of *Winning Her Business: How to Transform the Customer Experience for the World's Most Powerful Consumers*:

> *'When product launches fail, it's often because consumers' real-life perspectives were not included in the strategic development phases, from R&D to marketing. Inclusivity is a powerful solution to this issue.'*

* * *

The first opportunity for your brand to boost profits is to ensure you're avoiding these seven costly mistakes. Improve your brand's performance by undertaking an audit of your current marketing activities and assess how many of these mistakes your business is making, and make a plan immediately for how you are going to address these problems.

Chapter 1: What have most brands been doing wrong?

- Don't treat mothers as one homogenous group.

- It's essential that board members remain well informed about trends and key changes within the mum market, and hold their senior marketers accountable.

- Don't pretend you know what mums want. Do your research and ask.

- Once relevance is lost, brands experience a very long, slow climb back. Mums don't forget quickly.

- Independent research, ensuring you have mums on all your external teams, and keeping control of your strategy are critical to success.

- Involve mums in your new product development.

KEY POINTS

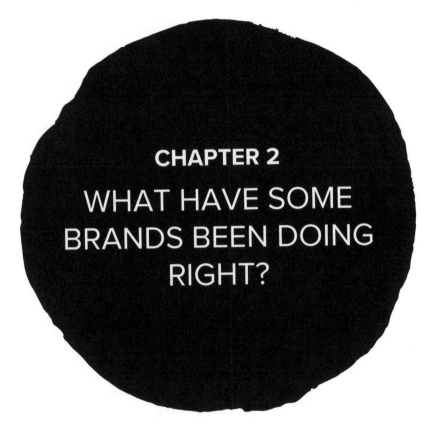

CHAPTER 2

WHAT HAVE SOME BRANDS BEEN DOING RIGHT?

It's certainly not all doom and gloom. There are some wonderful examples of brands that are highly successful at engaging mothers, which is leading them to enjoy market share gains. Mothers will gravitate towards brands that can show they understand what mums need and what they have to deal with every day, and how tough it is to be a mother. In many of these brands I see the following six strategies being used well:

1. Being different and standing out to mums.

2. Understanding diversity and the modern family.

3. Telling compelling stories.

4. Showing empathy for mums.

5. Communicating in a fun and playful way.

6. Providing surprise and delight.

Let's have a look at each of these.

Strategy #1: Being different and standing out to mums

One of the most effective methods of breaking through the marketing noise for mothers is being different, whether that's innovation in product offerings or standing out with marketing communications. Brands are being rewarded by mothers for taking a unique approach, and if that difference includes being more playful and humorous then the rewards can be even greater.

ALDI has recently been named Australia's most trusted brand by Roy Morgan, an incredible achievement given they only moved into this highly competitive market dominated by two major supermarket retailers in 2001.[1] ALDI lives by its 'Good Different' strategy. Not only do they help families save money on their groceries, they

---

1 www.roymorgan.com/findings/7755-net-trust-score-general-brands-201811200006.

also focus heavily on their offers for mothers. For example, they are well known for their baby products and the removal of artificial colours from their products to help families instil a healthy lifestyle. They also cater to the growing trend towards protecting the environment, removing environmentally damaging micro-beads (which are commonly used in toothpastes and beauty products) from all their products. And ALDI's laundry products have no phosphates, to help keep Australian waterways clean.

These examples position ALDI as doing things differently from the two other major supermarket retailers. They are offering an alternative when previously the market didn't feel there was one.

As well as their family-friendly products, the way in which ALDI speaks to their customers really resonates with mothers. ALDI uses a playful and fun approach to supermarket shopping, which is usually seen as a tedious chore. Perhaps their advertisement that resonates most strongly with mothers is the dancing shopping trolley: we see a woman perform a dance routine with her shopping trolley as she returns it to the trolley bay. I surveyed mothers across the country after this ad launched and there was unanimous praise for making the mundane fun again.

Despite such successes, I'm seeing fewer senior marketing executives willing to take risks in recent years. They feel the growing pressure to demonstrate short-term return on investment, and so are opting for safer options so as not to slow their next career move. This is resulting in a glut of 'same same' for mothers, and as a result they are increasingly disengaging. This opens up the opportunity for your business to separate itself from your competitors.

Strategy #2: Understanding diversity and the modern family

Some brands are enjoying great success by recognising that mums want more diversity in their marketing communications.

In the UK, 65% of families are non-traditional. Volvo really harnessed this insight and produced the 'Family Icons' video that focused on reflecting changing family structures, including women who had their first child in their 40s, same-sex couples and blended families.[1] They partnered with a Westfield London in Shepherds Bush to challenge the existing imagery of parenthood and celebrate increasingly diverse family structures. Together they redesigned the family parking bay imagery in their car park to include new signs for same-sex couples with a baby, single mothers with a baby and two sets of parents with a baby. Not surprisingly, it was very well received by mothers and families, and positioned Volvo as being customer-centric and demonstrated a deep understanding of modern parenthood.

Another great example of brand success through embracing diversity is Tylenol. They embrace diversity in every part of their organisation. It has become a core value for the company, and this shines through in their marketing. Their #HowWeFamily campaign has been running since 2015 and celebrates all the different ways people form families. They have positioned their brand as being inclusive of all different family structures – such as same-sex, inter-racial and blended families – to demonstrate how their brand helps all types of families.

Strategy #3: Telling compelling stories

Stories have the great ability to humanise your brand. Mums especially are emotive and connect with stories, and are rejecting traditional corporate sales messages. Stories are a great way to attract mums and build a relationship with them.

Your 'brand story' can be powerful and influential. This is the first story you want to really get right. This is the story of why you

---

1   https://vimeo.com/278654070

do what you do, the values your company has, and the reasons behind the products and services you have created for mums.

You can then also create stories for individual products. For example, in Australia Hyundai has successfully created rapport with parents by focusing on the story of kids fighting in the back-seat of the car to promote its Santa Fe car model.[1] They depict familiar mini-stories of kids fighting on the back seat of the car and the stress it causes parents while driving. We travel through time from the 1950s through to modern times, seeing familiar fights break out between siblings travelling on the back seat. Santa Fe promises peace to parents, highlighting how their new car technology and design features will settle the back-seat fighting once and for all. They have successfully used storytelling to demonstrate their understanding of the pain point of driving with the family – children fighting – and used this to show their new product features, which will satisfy the kids and keep the peace.

Strategy #4: Showing empathy for mums

Empathy is an incredibly effective tool for building a deep, lasting relationship with mothers. In our Marketing to Mums research, mums repeatedly made it clear they feel a disconnect between advertising and their reality. They expressed a desire for market-ers to stop portraying perfect lives with mothers who have it all together, because it's just not the life they are leading. It is not one they are aspiring to either. They feel like their lives are being trivi-alised and so they dismiss the brand's marketing messages.

There is often an aversion to strongly stylised communications that assume mothers are highly aspirational when in fact the vast majority of mothers are looking for authenticity. They are looking

---

1 www.youtube.com/watch?v=I2I7HybrgfA

for cues that brands understand the complexity of their lives. Brands that accurately depict the reality of their lives are richly rewarded.

Mums have made it clear they want marketers to respect them and earn their attention. Mothers across the world want to be treated as women first, mothers second. Motherhood is important to them, but it is not *all* of them, and they want to be respected for the multi-dimensional people that they are.

Empathy in your marketing starts with deeply understanding your core segment of the mum market through research. However, it's not enough to know them; mums want you to demonstrate a deep *understanding* of them. When this is achieved, rapport is quickly built.

A great example of successfully using empathy is the Yoplait 'Mom On' commercial from 2017, which tackles the issue of mothers feeling judged for their choices. Whether that choice be breastfeeding in public, going back to work, having a child later in life, wearing lycra or using bribery to get their children to participate in chores around the house, Yoplait depicts the ongoing daily judgements mums feel they are up against. This commercial successfully positioned the Yoplait brand as having a deep understanding and empathy for the constant judgements mums feel, including the choice of what they choose to feed their child.

In Australia, a global athleisure brand called Active Truth is another great example. This business was started by two mothers who identified that most big brands' designs didn't work well for pregnant women, nor did they work well for women sized 14 or over. So they have created a clothes range specifically for pregnant women and mothers who want something very functional. They recognised that pregnant women really wanted tights that weren't going to roll down their bump. They saw that mothers were seeking tights that would hold them in the right places, were extremely comfortable, and also allowed them to store their phone and keys. They offer inclusive sizing, and believe all women deserve to look and feel great in activewear that fits, flatters and supports through every stage of life. Active Truth celebrates diversity and refuses to modify the images of their models, challenging stereotypes and biases around body image. In three short years they are seeing great success. Being real and respecting and empathising with mothers has seen them embraced by the market and they have built a very healthy online business, selling over 50,000 pairs of tights.

On a political level, Jacinda Ardern, the New Zealand Prime Minister, is winning international admiration from many, but most significantly with mothers. She is something of a pin-up girl for modern mums. They love how she demonstrates that mothers can have many dimensions; be a prime minister, a mother, a partner, a friend. Her feminine leadership speaks very strongly to women. Her ability to demonstrate deep empathy during a terrorism incident in New Zealand won her deep support. And her 2019 'wellbeing budget' – which focused on poverty, homelessness and mental illness – has only strengthened their admiration for this leader.

Strategy #5: Communicating in a fun and playful way

Mums worry. Mums are solving problems all day long. They are making decisions for themselves, their children, their partner and, often, their aging parents. Life can feel a bit serious. As such, in our Marketing to Mums research we found mums asking for more playful communications from brands. Companies that really gained their attention on an ongoing basis made things 'a bit fun'.

'Make advertising fun and interesting. It seems the standard "everyone in the same box" approach is boring and outdated. Time to get creative!'

Marketing to Mums survey (2019)

A great example of this is Clorox in the US, which makes cleaning products. They produced a series of YouTube pre-rolls (the short promotional video which runs prior to the actual video selected) aimed at mothers. They clearly understand mothers face some unique experiences with their children every day, and they share a selection of these more memorable moments to make mums smile. The video quickly cuts through the marketing noise and builds rapport among their core shopper segment. In one pre-roll video we see mum walk in on her son who is playing a game with his friend in the bathroom. There is tape stuck on the floor, some distance from the toilet. When the mother questions why the tape is on the floor, she is informed they are having a contest to see who could reach the toilet from the furthest point. In another pre-roll video, Clorox shows a small child who is helping out around the house by mopping the bathroom floor. We then see he is 'rinsing' the mop in the toilet.

Clorox used a strategy of fun, playful communications to highlight 'life's bleachable moments'. The reactions when I show these pre-rolls during my speaking engagements include *'who would have thought that buying bleach could be so much fun'* and *'I will never forget that brand'*. Fun and playful communications can successfully make a brand memorable in a positive way.

Celeste Barber is a trained actor, writer, comedian and mother who hit international fame for recreating the often ridiculous poses made by many models, celebrities and influencers under the hashtag #celestechallengeaccepted. These amusing parodies also point to a disturbing portrayal of celebrity women in media. Starting in early 2015, Barber has built a following of more than seven million global fans across Facebook and Instagram, many of whom are mums, and she has become an influencer in her own right, touring the US and Europe, landing the cover of *InStyle* magazine, and launching a book. This notoriety has led her to start co-creating content with brands across the world, allowing brands to successfully tap into playful communications to gain strong awareness and build rapport with women. In Australia, Barber has worked with Holden, an automotive brand, to demonstrate their Equinox model's functionality. In this national commercial, Barber is depicted as an international superstar draped over the car and working with a top French director. Mothers were unanimous in their love of the advertisement, with one mum saying:

> 'Nailed it! This is truly awesome. It made me genuinely warm to the car and the brand. Kudos to the Holden marketing team for having the guts to run with a "real" mum. It's so much better than any other car ad.'

Barber has gone on to work in the US and collaborated with the likes of Tom Ford, allowing brands to demonstrate that they don't take themselves too seriously and so gain further credibility.

In Australia in the FMCG (fast-moving consumer goods) industry, McCain has released a playful campaign. The 'Oh My Veg' campaign features a couple in a counselling session discussing the female partner's 'exotic tastes' while her male partner 'prefers peas'. It's a fun and entertaining ad campaign which asks shoppers to rethink the frozen vegetables category as it promises to deliver unexpected tasty combinations.

In France, hypermarket retailer E.Leclerc received a great response to their advertisement that led with humour. The commercial shows a woman discovering she is pregnant and, as she shares the news with her partner, we see him terrified by the impending costs he foresees with raising a child. The retailer is there to support him with lower cost household goods.

Humour can be a very effective tool to cut through all the white noise mums feel they are inundated by.

Strategy #6: Providing surprise and delight

Surprise and delight can be a very effective strategy for engaging with mums. Providing a mother with a surprise can let her know how important and special she is. My Marketing to Mums research reveals that mothers feel it's the little personalised touches that can influence them to choose one brand over another.

I asked Amy Henry, President of FlashLight Insights in Philadelphia and strong advocate for surprise and delight as a strategy, to explain the benefits:

'When brands engage in surprise and delight, they do far more than catch mums' attention. What separates a surprise and delight strategy from a gimmick is that essential insight that tells her:

1. *I've anticipated what you want because I'm really paying attention.*

2. *I see our relationship as more than just transactional.*

3. *I don't take your business or loyalty for granted.*

4. *I believe you are a person deserving of joy.*

'So, it's no surprise that brands that surprise and delight feel more human than brands that do not. They are lovable, but also forgivable if they fall a step behind or make a mistake. Surprise and delight strengthens brands in the short term and makes them stand the test of time (and competitors, and missteps, and even the occasional misjudgement).'

Amy cites JetBlue, a low-cost US-based airline which used surprise and delight to highlight to mothers that they understood the judgement they faced when travelling with a baby. It was part of their activities to celebrate mothers for Mother's Day. They released a three-minute YouTube video called 'FlyBabies', which took us through four mothers' preparation for a flight with their baby from New York to Long Beach. It highlighted the stress and anxiety of travelling solo with a baby. As the flight takes to the air the stewardess welcomes people to the first and only FlyBabies flight, where a crying baby 'is a good thing'. People on the flight were told they would receive a 25% discount off their next JetBlue flight for each crying baby on the flight, so a total of four crying babies meant they would receive a free flight. Immediately, the four women could relax, and there were immense celebrations when the fourth baby cried.

JetBlue were aiming to get passengers to have greater empathy for parents travelling with a small child with the message 'next time, smile at a crying baby for crying out loud'. While this was a one-off publicity stunt on a real flight, it served to build stronger relationships among US mothers who felt that JetBlue understood them. It clearly highlights that JetBlue understand mothers, and the surprise and delight element of this marketing activity which saw them receive a free JetBlue flight really challenged passengers to rethink travelling with babies on a flight.

ALDI Australia also uses surprise and delight with their weekly 'special buys'. One week a customer might discover significantly discounted skiwear, while the next week you might find all your camping needs. Each week is a new surprise, and brings some discovery opportunities to make the grocery shopping experience less boring, while also delivering enormous sales opportunities for ALDI. Long queues outside stores on the launch of 'ski week' special buys are not uncommon as mums share the news via social media.

As Mita Mallick, Head of Diversity and Cross Cultural Marketing at Unilever North America, suggests:

'Let's not perpetuate stereotypes. Let's deeply understand the different experiences of moms in order to surprise and delight them with products and services they never expected.'

There are great benefits for brands that use surprise and delight as a strategy. I have a client who is turning over $7 million per annum in a gourmet meal kit delivery business called Dinner Twist. Every delivery is a surprise in what the family will be eating that week. The entire family can often crowd around the delivery box, anticipating what will be in the recipe book this week. It saves parents time in planning what to cook each night, with the added convenience of not having to shop for the ingredients. And even with a high-growth business, this business owner still manages to call new clients on a weekly or monthly basis. Known as his 'happy calls', this allows him to surprise and delight his new customers and gain feedback about the product offering. Importantly, it allows him to stay deeply connected with his customers so the business can remain relevant and respond to market changes.

* * *

These six strategies are proving highly effective for brands seeking a competitive advantage. The success of these strategies is in brands having a deep understanding of their segment of the mum market they are seeking to attract. In the brand examples discussed in this chapter, they have clearly communicated to their mum segments that they understand them and this is being rewarded by mothers at the checkout. How well do you know your segment of the mum market? And more importantly, how well do they know your brand?

Chapter 2: What have some brands been doing right?

- Brands are being rewarded by mothers for taking a unique approach.

- Some brands are enjoying great success by recognising that mums want more diversity in their marketing communications.

- Stories are a great way to attract mums and build a relationship with them.

- Empathy is an incredibly effective tool for building a deep, lasting relationship with mothers.

- Humour can be a very effective tool to cut through all the white noise mums feel they are inundated by.

- Providing a mother with a surprise can let her know how important and special she is.

KEY POINTS

CHAPTER 3

MAJOR MUM TRENDS THAT WILL BOOST YOUR BUSINESS

There are a number of trends emerging that brands can harness to help gain growth for their brand. As Mita Mallick – Head of Diversity and Cross Cultural Marketing at Unilever North America – states:

'There are so many trends in the marketplace. Our job as marketers is to stay close to them. Women making the choice to have children on their own. Women choosing to have kids later in life. Women choosing not to become mothers. More men choosing to stay home and help raise their families, sharing the burden with working mothers. All of these trends and more are important for brands to watch to see how they can better serve these mothers and capitalize on these opportunities.'

In this chapter are seven trends that don't get the attention they deserve but which will really assist in your business developing an edge against other players in the market. These trends are:

1. The power of testimonials.

2. Convenience and time being valued at a premium.

3. Mums supporting female-owned businesses.

4. Audio is making waves.

5. Diversity is an expectation.

6. Minimalism is the new black.

7. The increasing role of dads, kids and grandmas in buying decisions.

Let's look at these trends that can help to dramatically grow your business if you get on board.

Trend #1: The power of testimonials

Mothers are increasingly rejecting corporate sales messages in favour of third-party endorsements. As they seek the perfect solution to their problem they use testimonials to refine their search and minimise the chance of making the wrong purchase decision. In our Marketing to Mums research in 2016 and again in 2019, we found testimonials to have the greatest influence in making a purchase – they even outperform a mum-to-mum recommendation. The sentiments from mothers in our research included:

> 'Testimonials are big for me, especially when the content isn't edited, with the good and perhaps not-so-good included. I would happily spend more on an item if I can read an honest review.'

> 'I find reviews the most helpful when researching a product or service for our baby. Hearing the pros and cons from people in the same position as me is a big influence for us. Incorporating reviews into each individual product you have on your site would absolutely increase the likelihood of me making a purchase.'

> 'Provide all feedback from previous buyers, not just positive five-star reviews; that way I don't have to search Google for hours to feel comfortable with the information. More often than not I will still purchase the product, and won't be surprised by the item having flaws. Not everything is perfect.'

Mothers understand that not everything is perfect all the time. They spend their days problem solving. And a bad review provides a great opportunity for brands to demonstrate how they handle a problem. Mums watch closely when this occurs.

It's critical that your brand invests in developing an effective testimonial strategy so mothers can easily source third-party endorsements to ensure your brand features in their consideration set. The influence of testimonials has led to the introduction of websites such as Tell Me Baby, a product review site operating in Australia and China which aims to be the TripAdvisor for baby products, helping parents seek out genuine reviews before making a purchase.

I've experienced the power of testimonials firsthand. A woman who owned a party supplies business read my first book *Marketing to Mums: How to sell more to Australia's most powerful consumer* and posted a review in a Facebook group for mothers in business. The post attracted a lot of attention about the practical steps I provided for small business owners, and within 48 hours my book had gone to number one on Booktopia's Business Books chart, Australia's largest online bookstore. It remained in the top 10 for the next four weeks. This book is now in its fifth reprint.

Testimonials are definitely powerful when wanting to influence mothers.

Trend #2: Convenience and time being valued at a premium

As the demands and expectations of mothers increase, so does the way they value convenience and time. Mothers are willing to pay a premium for greater convenience, and this is only increasing with the number of Millennials becoming mothers.

To understand this emerging trend more, I spoke with Wendy Liebmann, a respected retail expert and founder of WSL Strategic Retail. For 30 years her organisation has produced How America Shops® research, helping clients such as Walmart, L'Oréal, P&G and PepsiCo navigate the retail landscape in America:

'*Mothers are looking to make their lives easier, simpler. No surprise when you consider all the juggling they have to do. What is surprising is all the ways they are doing that, and the opportunities retailers and marketers now have to deliver stress-free, time-saving solutions to this audience that desperately needs some "me time" – and will pay for it.*

'Consider some of the things moms are doing in the US: shopping in more places to get what they need more efficiently. Yes, really. Gone are the days when they go to one place to buy everything under one roof. So often that's not efficient. It takes too much time. Often it's easier for moms to go to lots of place where they can get in and out fast. More is often less. And that's what they're looking to achieve. We call it "always all ready" to buy wherever they need it. Quick trips are growing fast. In-store and online.

'Other ways they're saving time are: using meal kits to prepare meals fast, using multi-functional products like vitamin-infused waters, and two-in-one beauty products (for example, moisturizer and foundation in one). And one dream many moms have is to gain time by cutting back on social media. (Unless of course they can "socialize" and buy all in one click.)'

One of the tasks where we are seeing convenience and efficiency gaining traction is outsourcing the shopping for clothing for children. For example, Kidbox is a subscription box of kids' clothing designed to help time-poor mothers who don't want to drag their child to the shops. Instead, a curated box of coordinated outfits is delivered on a seasonal basis – one more thing mums can tick off their long list of things to do. In 2019 Kidbox announced an exciting partnership with Walmart to offer a Kidbox subscription service via Walmart's online community, allowing the retailer to expand its online kids' apparel offering and providing a large distribution channel to Kidbox. This business has proven very successful because it understands that working mothers increasingly value their time, and they also enjoy the surprise and delight aspect of this shopping experience.

Trend #3: Mums supporting female-owned businesses

With mums entering business at an ever-increasing rate (in Australia, women are entering business at almost three times the rate of men and have been for more than a decade), we are seeing a strong trend of mothers wanting to support women in business. This is in part wanting to see the businesses succeed, but it is rooted in a deep dissatisfaction with the way they are currently not being recognised. It's a way for them to claim some of their economic power as a consumer and help address gender inequality. Directories have been set up – such as Purse Power in the US and Femeconomy in Australia – which require, for example, businesses to have 30% representation of women on the board or be 50% female owned to be listed. They act as a directory for women wanting to support women in business. They are gaining interest from women across the world, and should they gain critical mass will greatly reward brands with strong female board representation and ownership:

'I am absolutely passionate about buying from women who are creating a business for themselves and their families, and if I can get what I want from a girlfriend's business or a lady start up then I will every single time over a big, faceless company.'

'I have so much admiration for women putting themselves out there, taking a risk to build their future. It takes hard work and determination. If I can help support women in their business I would rather see my money go to help them in their journey.'

Marketing to Mums research (2019)

In India one of the biggest players in the baby space, FirstCry, is tapping into the growing trend of mothers wanting to support business ventures by mothers. Launched in 2010, FirstCry has more than 150 physical stores, with planned launches for another 100 stores and 300 pop-up stores. They have online dominance, with a Facebook community of more than two million mothers and 7.5 million registered website users. FirstCry has established a specific section on their website dedicated to supporting 'mumpreneur' brands. It is a unique way for a large brand to tap into this growing trend.

Trend #4: Audio is making waves

We are seeing a large rise in the popularity of podcasts, particularly among mums in business. As experienced multitaskers, mums are listening to podcasts while in the car, exercising, commuting to and from work, cooking, doing the laundry and sport runs – whenever they can get a moment. I interviewed Melissa DeCesare, VP at Edison Research, for the Marketing to Mums Podcast, and she shared insights from their 2019 'Moms and Media' study which found that 56% of US mothers have listened to a podcast.[1] The interest among mums in podcasts is strong across the world. Marketing to Mums has recently undertaken research into Australian mothers and their use of media and new technology. Having surveyed more than 650 mothers, we found 40% of Australian mothers had listened to a podcast in the past month alone.

Mums also love the intimacy of podcasts. They find them real, relatable and personal, and this all helps build trust for brands. Because they can be listened to on demand they are appealing to mums who want to use their time efficiently. Business podcasts are the most popular genre among mum business owners for development of skills and knowledge at a time convenient to them.

Speaking with mum of three and co-host and producer of the #BusinessAddicts podcast Loren Bartley, she believes mums in business are attracted to podcasts as they allow mums to get quick, actionable tips on their chosen topics on demand. Loren believes

---

1 www.edisonresearch.com/moms-and-media-2019

that mums are also attracted by being able to gain access to advisors and experts that they may otherwise not. Along with a strong interest in business podcasts, I also see mothers' interests being wide and varied, with general knowledge, parenting, spirituality, health, comedy and self-development also popular, reflecting the diverse nature of mums.

It's certainly something I've witnessed myself. In late 2018 I launched the world's first podcast for marketing professionals wanting to better understand how to improve their marketing to mothers. Debuting at number six on the Australian Apple Podcast Business Charts, it now has a strong listener base of female marketers.

Podcast clubs are starting to replace traditional book clubs. Australian business owner and mum of two Dr Leandra Brady-Walker is one of a growing number of mothers in Australia who are part of a podcast club. Each month one mum chooses a podcast which they all listen to, and then they get together and talk about it over cheese and wine. Mums are encouraged to listen to as many episodes as possible of that particular podcast. A different podcast genre is usually selected each month, providing rich discussions around different topics from feminism to wellness. Leandra enjoys the friendships she develops while learning new things and engaging in stimulating conversation.

One step further is Podcast Brunch Club, a website that brings together podcast listeners online and in person. Founded in Chicago by Adela Mizrachi, Podcast Brunch Club curates up to five hours of listening each month around a particular theme, and then members meet up across the world to discuss. They have more than 60 in-person meet ups each month across six continents.

Podcasts present a fantastic opportunity to build relationships with an engaged audience of mothers. Brands can connect with mums in an uncluttered and uninterrupted way that has none of the distractions of other advertising mediums.

There are three clear opportunities for brands to tap into the growing trend of mothers listening to podcasts. These are:

- appearing as a guest on a podcast
- sponsoring a podcast
- creating a podcast for your brand.

Being a guest on an established podcast to share your brand story is a low-cost method and a great entry point. There are agencies now established to assist brand leaders and business owners secure guest bookings and assist you to build your podcast strategy. Kelly Glover is the founder of The Talent Squad, a Podcast PR agency. After a 16-year career in radio she launched her business in 2017 to help brand leaders get booked onto podcast shows.

Sponsoring a podcast is also a great opportunity for your brand to be introduced to mothers by the podcast host; typically at the beginning, in the middle and at the end of the podcast. The commercial advantage of podcast sponsoring is significant, with a US research company reporting that 60% of respondents would prefer to buy from the companies that advertise on their favourite podcasts.[1]

Creating a podcast for your brand is the most involved option of the three but can be richly rewarding. Westpac, an Australian bank, is a big brand that has successfully launched a podcast for pregnant women. Called Hello Bump and hosted by Rebecca Judd and Monique Bowley, it takes listeners through their pregnancy journey month by month. We hear Bec Judd, a television presenter and mum of four, answer all those questions which no one tells you about. The podcast promotes the bank's Hello Bump initiative, where they deposit $200 into a Bump Saver account for newborns which is accessible when the child turns 16. The Hello Bump podcast has had over a million downloads since launching, and was

---

1   www.whooshkaa.com/faq

awarded Best Branded Podcast at the Australian Podcast Awards in 2018. The podcast has been so successful that Westpac have now launched 'The Split' podcast helping women navigate separation and divorce.

If you are targeting mums in business, podcasts are a growing trend you just can't ignore, but you should be jumping on this trend no matter what your target mum market. And many brands are. In fact, podcast ad spend is growing rapidly, and is forecast to exceed $1 billion in the US by 2021.[1] There are great opportunities for brands to embrace podcast advertising in its early days and reap significant rewards, namely mums' uninterrupted attention.

Trend #5: Diversity is an expectation

Diversity is increasingly an expectation of parents globally. While I've shown you some excellent examples of brands that have successfully embraced diversity, the majority of brands still fall short:

'One of the biggest mistakes is not understanding that moms are not a monolithic segment. We have to go beyond what has been long considered the perfect image of family; the traditional nuclear family, a mom and dad and two kids, and the particular role the mom plays in that family. Let's be inclusive of all forms of motherhood and families. Homes with a single mom, two moms, where grandmothers or aunts become the mother figure, working mothers and stay-at-home moms. We also have to understand the cultural nuances and differences when it comes to motherhood across cultures.'

Mita Mallick, Head of Diversity and Cross Cultural Marketing, Unilever North America

---

1 www.marketingdive.com/news/us-podcast-ad-spend-surged-53-in-2018-iab-and-pwc-find/556144/

In researching for this book, I've spoken extensively with Australian mothers and I continually heard the need for less stereotyping and for brands to be more inclusive of the changing family structure that exists now:

> 'Brands have the cookie-cutter mum look on every ad. But there are mums with coloured hair, tattoos or piercings. There are chronically ill mothers and mothers that are carers. Australia is a multicultural society, and there is a lot of support for the gay community; this should be incorporated in some way.'

> 'Mothers come in different sizes, races and ages. Often mothers are portrayed as young, white and slim. Often houses are shown as perfect, but that's not reality. I often feel that as an older mother with children aged from 5 to 24, I am not represented by the media.'

> 'Brands should get more mothers who use the product to tell their story, in a believable way. Also, a bit of colour in the adverts; we aren't all white, blonde mums and kids. A different face catches my attention. I'm over the whitewash of Australian media.'

> 'Brands need to realise that there are so many different types of mums (in fact sometimes dad is mum as well); mums that work, mums that don't, alternative lifestyles, not just the 1950s-style perfect mum with the tray of muffins and the apron.'

The expectation of diversity grows greater in younger generations. If you are not demonstrating diversity in your marketing communications with Generation Z mothers and younger Millennial mothers, you are risking your brand's credibility with these groups.

Trend #6: Minimalism is the new black

Mums are embracing minimalism as they opt to live simpler, more meaningful lives.

Respected global research firm GfK has revealed that mums feel more stress than any other consumer group, with typical stressors being:

- their weight

- their health

- lack of sleep

- the unwanted 'noise' of advertising that fills their lives.

These stresses are key drivers towards the minimalism movement, and this trend is having an especially significant impact on clothing and apparel brands.

In the past few years – particularly since decluttering guru Marie Kondo launched her book *The Life-Changing Magic of Tidying Up*, followed by the Netflix series in 2019 – mothers are actively choosing to buy less, particularly less clothing and shoes. They are aspiring to live more simply, and are adopting a 'less is more' approach to life. It's a clear protest to the busyness of the lives mothers now find themselves living, and a revolt against consumerism, fast fashion and waste.

Mums want to declutter and destress their minds and focus on what is really important to them. They want a simpler, sustainable life. They are starting to put greater consideration into every aspect of their lives, including who they spend time with and the things they purchase. They are adopting mindful decision making.

Sarah Bartholomeusz, an Australian mother of two and founder of You Legal, completed a self-imposed challenge in 2017 to buy no items of clothing for one year. Sarah wanted to transform her relationship with retail, and says she found the experience liberating.

She was able to downsize her wardrobe significantly and donate clothes she was no longer wearing to opportunity shops and her work clothes to a charity that helps women get back into the workforce. It also had a far-reaching impact on her views about retail spending in 2018 and beyond. Sarah has eliminated her instinct for purchasing clothes on a whim, and she intends to purchase fewer items, choosing only those of higher quality.

Sarah is not alone. Minimalism is becoming a movement for women across the globe. Facebook groups and influencers have popped up to support and encourage women to buy less, wear what they already have, and focus on what really matters to them. The number of mothers who aspire to these values is rapidly growing. It has led to the explosion of the share economy, where people swap, hire or share clothing and other items in a conscious effort to live with less.

Mums embracing minimalism are removing temptation by unsubscribing from shopping newsletters in droves. They are also actively unfriending brands on social media to focus on what's really important to them. This removes lots of the 'noise' they are subject to from brands and advertisers. When they do spend, it is a far more considered decision, and they opt for higher quality items. They are also looking for pieces of clothing that are not subject to fashion trends, opting for more classic styles. It's no wonder that fast fashion retailers are struggling, and we are seeing the demise of previously successful fashion retailers.

A new industry is emerging in their place; women are choosing to hire clothing and accessories more often. Mothers love the fact that they can hire a special piece of clothing for an event, party or special occasion, rather than having to purchase. Businesses across the globe – such as Rent the Runway in the US, Front Row in Europe, Girl Meets Dress in the UK and Her Wardrobe in Australia – are booming. This trend is unlikely to slow down. Gen Z are very high users of hiring (as part of the sharing economy

– see chapter 7 for more on this), and we are soon likely to see them demand this offering across many other categories also.

Trend #7: The increasing role of dads, kids and grandmas in buying decisions

Younger Millennial parents are adopting a more egalitarian approach to parenting. Millennial parents are entering parenthood on equal terms. We are also seeing kids and dads having more of a say in purchase decisions, with a more collaborative approach being taken in modern households. This is a significant shift which is having a big impact on high-value purchases, including the family car, houses and family holiday destinations. While mum's influence still dominates and she'll often make the decision, the thoughts of dad and the children are being considered. It's creating further complexities for brands.

I spoke with Michelle Poris – Vice President at Smarty Pants, a leading youth and family research and consulting firm based in the US – to get her views on this important shift:

'More than ever, today's kids are strongly influencing parents' purchase decisions. With their 24/7 access to unboxing videos, online shopping sites, Instagram posts, and more, kids have the latest and greatest new products at their fingertips, and are eager to share their opinions with parents. And parents count on their kids' opinions, for both kids' products and household/ family purchases. When buying something for their kids, parents would rather not waste money or time and instead prefer to purchase exactly what their child wants. But even for household or family purchases - whether food and beverage, home electronics, entertainment, a vacation destination, etc. - parents often seek their children's input, recognizing kids' valuable expertise as well as having an ultimate desire to make their kids happy.'

In a Marketing to Mums podcast interview with Jeff Fromm, President at Futurecast, he talked about this changing family dynamic, stating that approximately 25% of stay-at-home parents now are dads. This is having big implications for brands, as dads are increasingly taking responsibility for everyday household purchases. It's not surprising we are seeing real push back from mothers around the world, who are turned off by the depiction of dads as being incapable of caring for their children or as 'babysitting'. They will immediately discount your brand if you do this.

> 'My partner is just as involved in caring for our baby as me and the advertising for baby products excludes him and assumes I am a stay-at-home mum.'
>
> *Marketing to Mums survey (2019)*

With Generation Z listening to older influences, a distinct change from Millennials, we are also likely to see the influence of grandmothers increase. Last year I recorded a podcast interview with Patty David, Director of Consumer Insights at AARP, one of the largest not-for-profit membership-based organisations in the US, which is dedicated to empowering Americans aged 50-plus to choose how they live as they age. With a membership of more than 38 million people in the US, I knew she'd have some great insights into the role of grandmothers today. Patty painted a picture of a powerful, influential consumer who is increasingly getting involved in day-to-day family life and whose needs must be considered by marketers who want to influence the family household purchasing decisions.

* * *

For long-term success, brands must focus on creating deeper, more meaningful relationships with mothers, and to do this you must recognise and understand the trends in the mum market. Companies need to focus on the quality of their products and services to demonstrate real value. Demonstrating ethical sourcing also helps, as this goes hand-in-hand with the minimalism movement. This can only be achieved by taking the time to look at the changing trends of purchasing by mums and working to understand their needs and respond accordingly.

Chapter 3: Major mum trends that will boost your business

- Mothers are increasingly rejecting corporate sales messages in favour of third-party endorsements.

- Mothers are willing to pay a premium for greater convenience, and this is only increasing with the number of Millennials becoming mothers.

- With women entering business at an ever-increasing rate, there is a strong trend of mothers wanting to support women in business.

- Podcasts present a fantastic opportunity to build relationships with an engaged audience of mothers.

- If you are not demonstrating diversity in your marketing communications, you are risking your brand's credibility.

- Mums are embracing minimalism as they opt to live simpler, more meaningful lives.

- While mum's influence still dominates and she'll often make the decisions, the thoughts of dad and the children are being considered more now than in the past.

KEY POINTS

CHAPTER 4

THE BIG OPPORTUNITIES IN THE MUM MARKET

Opportunities abound for brand leaders who go looking. In this chapter I'm going to highlight eight significant opportunities within the market that can get you started on the road to big profits in the mum market. This list is by no means exhaustive; there are many other sub-segment opportunities, but these are the sub-segments that I feel are largely ignored, poorly addressed, or represent the fastest growth possibilities:

1. Invisible mums.

2. Single and solo mums.

3. Tech-first mums.

4. Generation Z mums.

5. Mum-led businesses.

6. Migrant mums.

7. Pregnant women and first-time mums.

8. Grandmothers.

Of course, there are further distinguishing behaviours to delve into within these categories, but I have hopefully captured enough to spark your interest and to get you started on your own research into these opportunities. I'm not pigeonholing mothers; these group-ings require further exploration. Demographics isn't everything. It's just the starting point.

Opportunity #1: Invisible mums

Women over 45 who are working and balancing the needs of dependent older children and the increasing health needs of their aging parents feel overlooked by the media and brands. They feel as though they are 'invisible mums', our Marketing to Mums research has revealed. Despite often controlling the finances of three generations – their children, their parents, and themselves – these women say they are rarely seen in advertising let alone catered for with services and products they may want. Marketers are missing out on an increasingly affluent shopper who holds great influence over spending.

The frustration of these women is well captured by one of our Marketing to Mums #inmumswords community participants, who says:

'I have four children. The youngest is now 14. There are many assumptions made about mothers with younger children being time poor and yes, that was a challenge, but the demands on your time as a mother with teenagers is extreme and I feel is misrepresented. Coupled with the fact that I also have aging parents to look after and a business, I don't feel us older mothers are well represented in the media nor are the demands on our time really understood. I am no longer in touch with other mums on a regular basis, primary school pick-ups are over, and I rarely have time to catch up with my friends these days who also all have teenagers. Thankfully some of my kids can now drive themselves, but I am still in the car all the time and this is where I do most of my shopping, in the car park waiting for a lesson to end. I am so infuriated by websites that are not mobile friendly and make navigating the site in order to purchase a chore. If more businesses actually had a device-friendly website, they would be going a long way to making me happier.'

These mothers are calling for brands to represent them in their advertising. They want brands to open their eyes and take the time to get to know them and truly understand their challenges. They want brands to better cater for their needs. As the world faces a growing aging population and kids staying at home longer, this consumer segment will grow significantly in coming years.

Their buying power cannot be ignored, and they want to be seen and have their needs catered for.

This view is echoed by Liz O'Donnell, whom I met at the M2Moms® – the Marketing to Moms conference in New York in 2016. Liz shared her own personal journey in her presentation 'Life in the Sandwich – the new care economy'. Liz is an author, speaker and founder of Working Daughter, which supports women balancing caring for an aging parent with a career. She said that of the 44 million family caregivers in America, 60% were women, often mothers, as society still expected that daughters do this work. She notes that we are now seeing the rise of the care economy, with the aging Baby Boomers, and with women in their late 40s and 50s increasingly dropping out of the workforce and dealing with illnesses, loss and grief.

She felt that marketers need to understand the following things about this growing consumer segment …

They are influencing technical innovation

O'Donnell spoke about the growing need for technical products which assisted her to communicate with her parents and her children and to schedule appointments and reminders when a parent required their medication or needed to attend a medical appointment.

They are looking for reliable services

Many of the Baby Boomers are wanting to stay at home as it becomes increasingly difficult to secure nursing facilities. O'Donnell spoke of the lack of services such as non-textured, nutritionally sound meals for her parents.

They need on-demand services

O'Donnell suggested these services might include an Uber-style offering specifically for getting kids to and from their after-school activities and weekend sport commitments to assist in lightening mum's load. She also spoke of services that accommodated wheel-chairs or immobile parents to transport to medical appointments when the carer was unable to do so.

They need support and TLC

More than anything, O'Donnell pointed to the lack of support for mothers experiencing the pressure of aging parents while juggling their own children and career. She spoke of the isolation, grief and loss many of them experienced. O'Donnell – an author, speaker and PR executive – started a new business to help facilitate the self-care she felt was so absent in her own experience.

* * *

50 is the new 30

I have firsthand experience being an invisible mum. I'm 48, but I don't feel 'middle-aged'; I feel as though I'm just coming into my prime. Since turning 40, I've become an award-winning international speaker, launched two successful businesses, written a bestselling book, launched a world-first podcast and am planning an international move once my three teenagers finish high school.

I feel as though I'm living a very different 'middle-aged' life to the generations before me, and it seems many women my age agree. A study of more than 500 women by UK-based marketing agency SuperHuman found that 96% of women over 40 didn't associate with being middle-aged either, yet marketing to women my age is still aimed at an outdated concept of what being middle-aged means. Today's women don't feel old.

So why are brands failing these women so badly? I asked some women in our #inmumswords community for their opinions and found them outraged:

'I'm not old. Don't they know 50 is the new 30?'

'*Pick up a magazine as a woman 60-plus in a hair salon and you would be forgiven for believing the only people in the world are stick thin, aged under 22, living a life of utter luxury. It's ludicrous. These emaciated girls and boys exist only in modelling agencies and yet they are the icons for all advertising from holidays to cars, from make-up to jewellery. Seriously, marketers, get over yourselves. I have been mad about this for years.*'

'*I now earn a lot, spend a lot, travel a lot and buy and sell property a lot, yet I only see myself represented as an exasperated stay-at-home mum of messy teenagers.*'

'*I don't think they've caught up with the idea that not everyone has kids in their 20s and older mums are still juggling kids and teens well into their 50s. Most over-50 advertising is aimed at empty nesters. So, while some may have extra disposable income, many of us are still up to our eyeballs in mortgages, music lessons, school fees. However, there is something about turning 50 that is a wake-up call to claim some of yourself back ... to live those crazy dreams and take better care of yourself. And there's not a lot of that promoted.*'

In fact, invisible mums were the most dissatisfied segment of our Marketing to Mums study of 1800 Australian mums. It's not surprising then to find out that 94% of the advertising industry is under 50 years of age.[1] The industry lacks empathy for these women. In a marketing environment that is increasingly competitive, this affluent group of women over 45 years are a missed opportunity.

What can brands do?

Recognising these women and featuring them in your creative will go a long way. I believe it starts with reviewing your marketing communications objectively. They are a digitally savvy group who

---

1 www.adnews.com.au/news/age-is-the-new-diversity-problem-in-advertising

are cashed up with little to buy. These women are significantly healthier, wealthier and more vital than women of their age from previous generations. These women are not old – many of them feel like they are just getting started.

Perhaps the most important finding here is the economic power of these invisible mothers. They are key influencers in all decisions across three generations. There is a clear opportunity for brands to ensure invisible mums are seen and heard. Be the first to cater to this market, include them in advertising and create products to assist and support them and be the first to reap the financial rewards.

The first step is eliminating ageism within your teams and supporting agencies. Look at developing training, or bring in a specialist to remove any unconscious bias held within your teams.

Be exceptionally careful with your choice of imagery. Stock photos will get you nowhere when communicating with this group, so I highly recommend investing in creating your own. It will immediately distinguish your brand from competitors. Invest in deeply understanding the unmet needs this segment can share with your brand. They will guide you to the opportunities and, in many cases, assist you to develop better products and services.

Opportunity #2: Single and solo mums

There have never been more single mothers in the world than right now. There are 320 million children across the world who live in a single-parent household, with the majority of these headed by women. Single mums have emerged as a powerful segment who are overlooked by most brands.

The size of the single-mother market is growing, particularly in western countries where being a sole parent is seen as more acceptable. Across the US, UK and Australia there are more than 14 million single-parent families, and 80% to 90% of these households are led by mothers, meaning there are well over 11 million single mothers in these three countries alone. The growing number of single and solo mothers in developed countries is largely due to increasing divorce rates, relationship breakdowns and women actively choosing to have children without a partner.

In the US, Pew research reports that 24% of mums are single mothers.[1] In a growing trend, Millennial single mothers represent the largest segment among all single mothers in the US, and black mothers are four times more likely to be single.[2,3] In fact, 61% of births to Millennials in the US are to single mothers.[4] In Canada and Germany, figures show one in five families have single parents. Like most countries, the vast majority of these are headed by mothers.[5] With statistics like this, single mothers can no longer be ignored.

The size of the single-mother market in Asian countries is harder to assess. Being single with a child in an Asian country is largely taboo. Bloomberg reported that single-mother households in Japan have increased 50% between 1992 and 2016.[6] In China many single mothers are fined and are unable to gain a hukou, an official document certifying that their child is a legal resident of their area.[7] In Asian countries these women can endure great financial hardship and societal discrimination, meaning that the real opportunity lies in western countries.

---

1   www.pewresearch.org/fact-tank/2019/05/08/facts-about-u-s-mothers/
2   www.pewresearch.org/fact-tank/2017/09/06/5-facts-about-millennial-households/
3   www.forbes.com/sites/christinecarter/2019/05/31/despite-the-odds-educated-single-black-mothers-are-dominating-corporate-america/#4a518ecf8b10
4   www.m2moms.com/fast-facts/
5   www.thelocal.de/20170413/single-parents-cant-live-off-full-time-minimum-wage-jobs-alone-report
6   www.bloomberg.com/news/features/2018-06-24/the-children-of-japan-s-single-mothers-are-living-in-poverty
7   www.chinapartnership.org/blog/2019/3/single-mothers-the-invisible-group-of-chinese-society

To help you better understand this growing segment and turn it into a profitable market for your business, let's have a closer look at single mums.

Single mums have growing financial empowerment

Single mothers are often very focused on raising healthy, well-adjusted children who understand the value of money. They tend to be excellent at budgeting as, in many cases, they've needed to be. They are attracted to educating themselves about financial matters and seek financial empowerment. They want their children to develop strong financial skills in case they ever find themselves as a single parent, and make enormous sacrifices to achieve this.

I grew up with a single mother and this rings very true to me. My mother returned to school after separating from my father. She became a typing teacher at a secondary college in the southern suburbs of Perth in Western Australia. She was determined that I understood the value of money as a child. It was important to her that she raise a financially independent child. She had me working from the age of 12. Each day after school I would walk up to the local golf course and pick up the balls off the fairway for $2 – every single day!

As soon as I entered high school I was educated about forecasting and budgeting. Each term throughout high school I had to submit a report to my mum with all my projected expenses, including uniforms, school books, excursions and pocket money. Once my budget was accepted I'd be given the money, and it was my responsibility to manage it over the term. So, while most 13 year olds were worrying about what to do on the weekend, I was stressing out about my cashflow. I understood it was very different at the time – it wasn't something that *any* of my friends were doing, but this difference has led to my success in life. My mum took great delight in handing over these reports to my fiancé at our engagement party to demonstrate I was fiscally sound and would be looking after the household finances. My mum's very different approach to parenting has seen me have a very good understanding of money: how to make, manage and save it.

There are two stand out examples of businesses that demonstrate a deep understanding of single mothers and resonate strongly with them. They both speak around financial empowerment. In Australia, Scott Pape, author of *The Barefoot Investor*, shares his tips on how to get financially stable with his step-by-step guide. He is empowering single mothers across Australia with practical information to increase their financial literacy, and assists them to rebuild their wealth so they can provide for their children. In the US, Emma Johnson from WealthySingleMommy.com has amassed the world's largest online community of professional single mothers. A respected business journalist and single mother herself, the WealthySingleMommy.com website receives 200,000 monthly page views, and her Facebook page has amassed more than 70,000 followers. She is also the author of the *New York Post* 'must read' book *The Kickass Single Mom* and appears as a solo parenting expert throughout the media.

Single mums are extraordinary jugglers

Single mothers are skilled jugglers. In the majority of cases they are working, running the household, overseeing childcare arrangements, play dates and sporting commitments, catching up with girlfriends, and possibly having a night out – all on their own. They are highly organised multitaskers because they need to be. It makes them incredibly efficient. And they are excellent employees as they know how to get things done.

Single mums have increasing entrepreneurial flair

Single mothers are establishing themselves as successful business owners. In Australia, Mums & Co, a community of mums in business, surveyed 852 mum-led businesses for the 'Australian

Mums in Business' report and found one in ten business owners are single mothers. Many chose to run a business to work around childcare needs.[1] Single mothers, however, are not limited to small business. We've seen many single mothers create highly successful larger businesses. In the US, Lisa Stone, a single mother of three, co-founded BlogHer, a media platform and series of events supporting female bloggers. Launched in 2005, it boasts an audience of more than 100 million women. In 2014 it was sold to SheKnows Media, and Lisa now focuses on a series of board and advisory appointments.

In Singapore, Kristie Lim, a single mother of four, founded Mind Stretcher, a series of 12 education centres across Singapore, after separating from her partner. Aged 33 and with her youngest child only one, she followed her passion for education, took a loan from her sister and plunged into working extremely long hours to build the business. She was persistent, resilient and determined. Sixteen years later, Mind Stretcher is a sought-after tuition brand in Singapore and has educated more than 200,000 children.[2]

In Australia, Cinzia Cozzolino was a single mother of two girls when she was confronted with a problem: her teenage daughter wouldn't eat breakfast. Being a nutritionist and understanding the importance of starting the day right, Cinzia set about finding another way to ensure her daughter received the nutrition she needed. Cinzia developed the Smoothie Bomb, a certified organic mix of 'superfoods' including nuts, seeds and dried fruits that could be added to a smoothie each morning which her daughter would happily drink. Word spread, and Cinzia found herself making these for friends and then cafés, before deciding she was going to turn this into a business. Smoothie Bombs are now sold in more than 600 stores across Australia and has a thriving online community.

1   mumsandco.com.au/insight/what-inspired-the-australian-mums-in-business-repo
2   sg.theasianparent.com/single-mum-successful-businesswoman-in-singapore

Cinzia's Smoothie Bombs have been a real hit with mums, and she is now turning over more than a million dollars each year – another incredible achievement from a single mum who was trying to solve the problem of getting her youngest daughter to eat breakfast. She credits her success to building strong retail channels alongside her online business. Smoothie Bombs are sold in eight overseas markets and they have recently been approached to be ranged in one of the biggest retailers in the US.

Ironically, her fussy-eating daughter now works alongside this innovative mum in growing the business!

What are brands getting wrong?

In speaking with single mothers, they are quick to point out a range of mistakes being made by brands. Brands fail to recognise their specific needs and challenges. The most common mistake is assuming their needs are the same as dual-parent families, as one of our #inmumswords community members explains:

> *'There's a baseline assumption that single-parent lives/ households run similarly to dual-parenting ones, which is fundamentally flawed ... because they cannot and do not.'*

Single mothers want to be acknowledged and understood:

> *'Take the time to understand us. Just ask.'*

> *'I'm not a typical mum. I'm older, single, financially secure, the sole decision maker and not freaked out when my bub sneezes, so a lot of advertising doesn't apply to me.'*

Single mothers and advertising

It's no surprise that single mothers are vastly overlooked in advertising. Research undertaken by Lloyds Banking Group in 2015 revealed that '19% of people featured in advertising were from minority groups and of that 19% a mere 0.29% were single parents'.[1] One brand recognising the huge opportunity this segment represents is IKEA. In 2017, IKEA tackled marketing to single mothers with their 'Where Life Happens' campaign in Sweden.[2] Their commercial depicts the reality of single life. The mother arrives home from work with her arms laden with groceries to find her three teenagers oblivious to the messy state of the house. Mum can hardly walk in the door over clothes, shoes and teenager 'stuff' all down the hallway. In exasperation, she drops her grocery bags and heads outside to get some air. Her teenagers do in fact notice this and start to clean up. The focus is the story of the real life of a single mother rather than product features. This approach resonates strongly with mothers who want brands to start depicting the reality of their day. The storytelling element creates connection and demonstrates the real understanding IKEA has of a single mother's life.

Brand considerations

Success will be delivered to brands that are harnessing these opportunities. Here are some tips to help your company do so:

- Invest in market research to deeply understand this segment. There is still much diversity within this segment and brands need to find and understand their niche.

- Upskill your marketing teams and educate them about this growing segment to explore how your brand can cater for their different requirements.

- Look for ways you can support single mums with greater convenience and time-saving options.

- Consider flexible payment options.

---

1 www.marketingweek.com/2016/12/06/lloyds-diversity-report/#
2 www.adweek.com/brand-marketing/ikea-explores-the-trials-of-single-parenting-in-its-latest-honest-take-on-family-life/

- Language and tone count when communicating with single mothers. Remember, they don't want your sympathy. Look to acknowledge and celebrate them in innovative ways.

The rise of solo mothers

A new sub-segment of the single mother market has emerged in western countries in recent years. Older, more affluent women in developed countries are choosing to enter motherhood without a partner. Known as 'solo mothers', these women are highly educated, financially independent, often have established careers, and are looking at adoption or donor insemination to become mothers. They typically have fewer children than dual-parent households, and this has an impact on their needs across a vast number of industries. They represent the most attractive sub-segment of the single mother market, but brands have yet to focus on this lucrative group.

So how do you connect with them? Solo mothers don't want sympathy. They've actively chosen to become parents. They want brands to stop using outdated stereotypes of what a solo mother looks like:

'I think there are a lot of misconceptions about the solo parent, namely that we are unhappy and/or struggling financially. I don't feel brands tap into my avatar, the mid-40s professional who chose to have a child solo and did so with a solid financial base.'

Solo mothers also want brands to acknowledge that they aren't co-parenting, so stress levels may well be higher and their need to invest time wisely is critical:

'Recognise us as a distinct demographic: educated, independent, financially savvy and usually time poor. We don't co-parent, so we never have any down time and therefore never put ourselves first. Make it convenient, but don't talk down to us, because that is so annoying.'

Mel Johnson is a woman from the UK in her late 30s who decided to become a solo mum after a relationship breakdown and the fear that she'd miss out on motherhood. At 39 she gave birth to a beautiful baby girl called Daisy. Since going through the donor insemination experience she has now launched a business around it supporting and advising other women who might be considering becoming a solo mother. She has a closed Facebook community, a podcast, and offers one-on-one coaching for women as they go through the process. Her website says:

> *'The Stork and I was created following my personal journey of having a baby on my own using donor sperm. It is dedicated to providing support and advice to others in similar situations.'*

Like all mothers, solo mums are diverse in their thoughts, behaviours and motivations.

Few brands are really addressing the needs of single mothers or the sub-segment solo mums, and this represents a strong growth opportunity for many brands across various sectors.

Opportunity #3: Tech-first mums

Today's mothers are looking for tech-first solutions to their problems. This starts with the smartphone. Australians are fast adopters of new technology. My organisation, Marketing to Mums, recently undertook a survey to better understand Australian mothers' media and technology preferences. The study was called 'Tech-first mums', and we found that 99% of 656 mums surveyed owned a smartphone. It's their most important tool for running their life and their family's life, and they pick it up 150 times each day.

Year on year we are seeing mothers spending more and more time on the internet, primarily via smartphones. This is where they start their buying research, so it's critical marketers are considering tech-first strategies to engage tech-first mothers early in their searches.

In the US, mothers are spending an extra 24 minutes on the internet compared to a year ago, and they are choosing a growing number of devices to do so. Millennial mothers are constantly adding to their technology choices. The 2019 'Moms and Media' report published by Edison Research and Triton Digital reveals a surge in tablet ownership by mothers over the previous 12 months; 75% of US mothers own a tablet, up from 64% the previous year.

The use of smart speakers is also growing. In the US, 34% of mothers own a smart speaker, an increase of almost five times since 2017. Amazon is the preferred option. It's a similar story in Australia, where 23% currently own a speaker and a further 13% are planning to purchase one soon, Google being the preferred option.

Wearable technology such as an Apple Watch is another technology product mums are adopting to help them stay connected. The 2019 'Moms and Media' research reported a significant rise from 10% in 2018 to 29% of US mothers having an internet-connected watch. Australia follows with 27% of mothers using wearable technology of any kind.

Mums are increasingly using ad blockers and are rejecting corporate sales messages, and favour media channels that support this. Our 2019 Marketing to Mums 'Tech-first Mums' research found Netflix to be extremely popular among mothers, with 51% of Australian mothers reporting watching Netflix in the past 24 hours. When queried about why they enjoyed Netflix, they talked about how they enjoyed the curated content, the 'me time' it delivered, and the absence of advertisements:

'It's like it knows me.'

'The choice is great and I can watch what I want when I want. So, if I have 10 minutes when I sit down for lunch I can pick up where I left off. No waiting for 8:30pm to come around every

*Wednesday to watch my fave show and then remember that
I have parent/teacher interviews.'*

*'It gives me the "me time" I need at the end of the night once the
kids are in bed.'*

*'It's all about portability and convenience here. I watch it on my
phone (the main reason I choose big phones) so I can feed my
addiction to multitasking.'*

*'Flexibility and deep diving when you have time. Watch it
on your phone, laptop or TV so I can multitask it with other
things like me doing manual prep in the warehouse or taking a
bath. I can watch with earphones in. It's smart enough to make
suggestions and it's so cheap for the whole family.'*

Tech-first mothers have high expectations of brands, and expect a seamless experience across digital devices with minimal clicks. They are increasingly adept at filtering content, so marketers have a limited amount of time to gain their attention. Once a brand has their attention, they expect brands to be accessible. They expect brands to know that they spend the bulk of their free time on mobile in the evenings after their children have gone to bed. Then they want to be able to converse with you. It's important that companies support this, and make it easy for mums with chatbots, social media messages enabled, and multiple other ways to reach you.

Tech-first mothers are also information seeking. Digital technologies have allowed them to develop impeccable research skills. In doing so, they've found some great shortcuts to get the information they want quickly and from trusted sources. They have access to multiple online communities which they tap into to get the information they need. In Australia in 2019, we uncovered that 80% of Australian mums belong to a closed Facebook group just for mums, up from 66% in our Marketing to Mums report three years ago. Tech-first mothers use social media to seek out other mums' opinions, and they look for a brand's social proof. They are searching for reviews, and awards a brand might have won.

A tech-first mother values efficiency and convenience. She is increasingly comfortable with online shopping, and services that speed up the sales and delivery process are well rewarded. She is willing to allow you to collect data if it will give her a better experience.

Tech-first mothers also have a global mindset. The internet enables them to buy from brands across the world. Does your brand allow international shopping, and do you have competitive shipping rates?

Tech-first mothers are sophisticated, savvy shoppers as technological advances have made them feel empowered, informed and better equipped than ever before to make savvy buying decisions. There's an opportunity for brands to be with their shoppers 24/7 in a way they haven't been able to in the past. Technological developments allow brands to be far more relevant and part of their lives.

Innovation and disruption

To learn more about tech-first mothers I spoke with David Butler, co-founder of Be Curious Partners, a venture capital firm focused on early-stage companies reinventing parenthood. David is the former VP, Innovation and Entrepreneurship at The Coca-Cola Company, working in a global role to lead disruptive innovation within the organisation, so he understands the disruption tech-first parents will bring to many industries. Be Curious Partners are obsessed with start-ups using tech to make it easier to be a new parent. Since launching in 2017 they've invested in many companies, including:

- Motherly, an online community of mothers sharing their experiences – makes it easier to be a new mum through its content and community dedicated to redefining motherhood.

- Kidbox, a subscription service of kids' clothing – makes it easier to shop for kids' clothes through its curated subscription service.

- Good Buy Gear, a high-quality secondhand website for children's clothing – makes it easier to buy or sell used gear (strollers, high chairs, and so on) online.

David says:

> 'The "parenting industry" hasn't changed much in the last few decades. Yet today's tech-first parents have vastly different expectations based on the tech-driven innovation happening in almost every other industry. And this is creating a new white space for innovation and entrepreneurship. As investors, we see a huge market forming around entrepreneurs who are using new tech to help solve age-old parenting problems – we've based our entire investing thesis around this belief.

> 'But we also feel this is changing dramatically. Today's Millennial parents are tech savvy. But tomorrow's Gen Z parents are tech natives. They spend an average of 10 hours online every day, have a much shorter attention span and are extremely comfortable multitasking. We believe "tech-enabled parenting" will continue to evolve with each new generation of parents.'

Brand considerations

How does your brand survive and thrive in an age of tech-first mothers? You can learn from successful businesses catering for the tech-first mother; for example, Parent TV, an on-demand video platform for parents, schools and childcare centres providing parenting information from worldwide parenting educators. It was started by Sam Jockel, an Australian mother of three who felt that mothers increasingly were unable to source the information they needed in the one location. Parent TV has an annual subscription and allows parents to access short two- to five-minute videos from leading global experts on a particular parenting topic. The absence of advertisements, coupled with the on-demand nature of delivery, is proving popular among tech-first mothers. Parent TV provides simple, effective strategies and advice to better support tech-first mothers. It enables video streaming of personalised parenting advice from the world's leading research-based parenting experts direct to parents via any digital device. A Millennial tech-first mother takes the role as a parent very seriously, more seriously than previous generations, and this platform allows her to educate herself on the challenges she is facing as she faces them, and satisfies her drive for education and self-improvement. Currently the service is catering for parents who have children aged up to 17 years and they have recently launched educational videos for children to watch on tricky topics parents are finding hard to talk to their children about.

Wearable technology products have real appeal to tech-first mothers. This has provided success for Clementine, an hypnotherapy app designed to help women feel calmer, believe in themselves and enjoy better sleep. It was launched in 2018 after its founder Kim Palmer experienced debilitating panic attacks at work and found hypnotherapy incredibly helpful. The Clementine app focuses on controlling the mind and helping women to adjust their mindset. It's been used by women going through challenging life experiences, including relationship breakdown, workplace stress and serious illness.

Peanut is a free friendship app which helps new mums find other like-minded mums. Founded in 2017 in the UK by Michelle Kennedy, a lawyer turned tech entrepreneur, and Greg Orlowski, co-founder of Deliveroo, it has amassed an audience of more than 650,000 mothers across the UK, US, Canada and Australia. Frequently called 'Tinder for mums', it solves the very real problem of loneliness and isolation faced in the early days of motherhood, which Michelle felt herself after the birth of her first child four years ago. The success of Peanut is underpinned by Michelle's deep understanding of modern new mothers who are seeking tech-first solutions to their problems. The app is built on the premise that not all mums are the same, and its algorithms will match you with mothers with similar interests to you, not just because you live in the same area. It is the ultimate resource and companion for modern motherhood, and allows mums to 'meet as mamas, connect as women'. It has proved incredibly popular among women with more than 100 million profile views and some 10 million messages between mums.

Kinedu is an award-winning app that provides parents with creative and age-appropriate activities to support a young child's development from birth up to four years of age. It's helping more than two million families across more than 180 countries. It provides daily play-based activities personalised to your baby, complete with progress updates. It also allows parents to record important developmental milestones, as well as giving access to articles written by education experts. Designed to empower parents to better understand their baby, it perfectly caters to the tech-first first-time parent, and has received well in excess of one million downloads. Kinedu has the capacity to collect significant amounts of data about early childhood development and compare and contrast this data across the world.

Innovation is critical in each of these successes. The companies have a deep understanding of the needs of this consumer. They understand that these women have grown up with tech, and they expect tech options to be available to them for parenting too.

Opportunity #4: Generation Z mums

Generation Z were born between 1996 and 2010, placing the oldest of Generation Z at 23 years of age at the time of writing. With the average age for having a first child being 23 in Indonesia, 26 in the US, 29 in the UK, 30 in France and 31 in Australia, there really is some urgency in understanding Generation Z mums right now.[1] By 2030, the majority of all births in the US will be to Generation Z women.[2] They have some behaviours that make them distinctly different from the Millennial mothers you might be attracting now, and as such they require a very different marketing strategy. If you want to stay relevant there are key characteristics you'll need to understand to adapt your strategy. Let's take a look …

Generation Z are hyper connected

Generation Z don't know a world without technology. Their digital aptitude is unprecedented, and being hyper connected is their norm. They are connected yet still isolated, as they spend more time on electronic media than in face-to-face interactions each day.

What is their device of choice? A US study by The Center for Generational Kinetics in 2018 found that young women were significantly more likely to use an iPhone (69%) than young men (52%).[3] We've seen similar results in our Marketing to Mums research in Australia, where mothers are skewed towards iPhone ownership. This has implications for app development and user experience priorities for brands. They also found Generation Z women used their phones for five or more hours a day more often than males (65% versus 50%). This has led Gen Z women to be far more connected with their friends than previous generations. A sense of community is vitally important to them.

---

1 https://www.huffingtonpost.co.uk/2016/03/09/pregnancy-around-the-world-age-of-new-mums_n_9416064.html
2 ifstudies.org/blog/a-snapshot-of-millennial-births
3 genhq.com/how-obsessed-is-gen-z-with-mobile-technology/

Generation Z is always 'on'

Pew Research reported in 2018 that 50% of US Generation Z teen-age girls are online 'almost constantly', compared to 39% of teenage boys.[1] This is almost double the results from their 2014–15 study. This level of hyper connectivity is likely to see them distracted, stressed and overwhelmed. The 2019 Junkee Media youth report uncovered that 71% of Gen Z women feel burnt out versus 55% of Gen Z men. Brands need to consider how they can better support these women, particularly in their transition into motherhood and beyond.

It's all about speed

Generation Z mothers are expected to be sophisticated, savvy shoppers. As a direct result of the technological advances available to them, they feel empowered, informed and better equipped than ever before to make savvy buying decisions. Gen Z mothers will value efficiency and convenience. They don't have time to waste. They are high users of on-demand services, and they seek to avoid advertising. Platforms such as Spotify Premium and Netflix prove particularly popular with this demographic. They love the curated content based on their previous selections as it allows efficient discovery of new content they will like.

There exists an opportunity to shorten the sales cycle among Generation Z mothers as they seek out efficient sales opportunities. I expect product review websites which also have ecommerce capabilities will be highly valued. They allow mothers to review what other mothers are saying about a particular product and place an order in one location, saving time.

Her user expectations are very high. She expects a seamless experience across digital devices with minimal clicks. It must be fast, easy to use and frictionless, with quick delivery of the product or service.

---

1 www.pewinternet.org/2018/05/31/teens-social-media-technology-2018/

Short attention spans

Generation Z mothers will filter content faster than any other generation we've seen. The younger the Generation Z mother, the higher her skills will be at filtering content. Not only do they use ad blockers at record levels but they scan now rather than read. I see this in my 16-year-old daughter. She doesn't 'read' a book but scans for keywords and puts the story together. This is a generation with a particularly short attention span.

I spoke with Jeff Fromm, President of Futurecast and co-author of *Marketing to Gen Z*, and he pointed out that this generation has grown up on short Snapchat videos and Instagram stories. They have been digesting 'snackable' pieces of content all their life. This has enormous implications for marketing communications, which must adapt. Jeff believes that brands need to focus on being direct, quick and simple in their approach with Generation Z mothers:

'These women are highly distracted. They seek snackable, short-form content from brands they follow.'

Social media shifts

Generation Z mothers will bring a shift in social media use as they favour Instagram, Snapchat and YouTube. In the US particularly, there is currently rapid take up of TikTok also. It's time to secure these social assets if you haven't already, and start upskilling your marketing team on their application. Facebook is not as important as it has been for generations of mothers before them. In fact, the younger Gen Z community have significantly less use for Facebook than older Gen Z people.

Generation Z are much heavier users of Instagram than previous generations. In Australia, I researched Gen Z between the ages of 12 and 17 and found that many had up to three Instagram accounts; one for their inner core of up to 30 friends, one public page for the hundreds (if not thousands) of people they did or didn't know, and a third account for their entrepreneurial side hustle. This third account was only found in the teenage girls I interviewed. In many cases this was an account they shared with a couple of other girlfriends, to rent out their party clothes or sell clothes they no longer wanted.

US researchers have made similar discoveries. In speaking with Michelle Poris, the Quant Savant from Smarty Pants, an esteemed market research company that specialises in the youth and family market, she shared results from their annual Brand Love Study with me and noted that they have seen a significant increase in the use of Instagram among tween girls over the past 12 months. This will have far-reaching effects when these girls become mothers. To ensure your brand doesn't miss this trend, your company needs to be preparing now for Instagram to become the dominant social media platform for mums.

YouTube is their preferred entertainment platform. YouTube influencers play an enormous role in influencing Generation Z purchase decisions, and should be a key consideration for brands. A 2015 Google study revealed that 70% of teenage YouTube subscribers find their favourite YouTube star is more relatable than traditional celebrities.[1] In Australian research undertaken by *Girlfriend* magazine, Editor Stacey Hicks said that Generation Z are far more likely to watch YouTubers live stream than TV.

YouTubers should definitely be a key media channel for brands, but keeping up with the changing tastes of YouTubers can be challenging. One only has to look at the recent fallout between two YouTube beauty influencers, Tati Westbrook and James Charles. Westbrook and Charles had been close friends, Charles even viewing Westbrook as an early mentor. But Westbrook posted a damning 40-minute vlog about her changed views about Charles

---

1 www.thinkwithgoogle.com/consumer-insights/youtube-stars-influence/

after he posted for a brand that was in competition to one of Westbrook's. Fans took sides, and within three days Charles had lost a staggering 3 million of his 16 million YouTube subscribers. By comparison, Westbrook more than doubled her subscribers from 5 million to more than 10 million. This is a great example of the depth of feeling about YouTube influencers and the consistent pivots Generation Z women can make.

Privacy is back

One of the key things that differentiates Millennials and Gen Z is privacy. Generation Z are far more conscious about what they disclose online. Privacy is far more important to them. Head over to a collection of Gen Z Instagram accounts and they are likely to be set to private mode. This will present challenges for brands in coming years; start thinking about this now as there will definitely be a shift towards more privacy compared to the current generation of mothers.

I spoke to Stacey Hicks, Editor and Content Director at *Girlfriend*, about Gen Z's desire for privacy, and she shared the following insight:

> 'Gen Z women have learned from their Millennial big sisters and take their privacy very seriously. They use social media to communicate rather than put their life on display online. Their number one priority is feeling good and they're open to brands and experiences that help them on their journey of self-discovery.'

Businesses such as Tinybeans – a photo and video sharing app – are well placed to cater for the Gen Z mother who values privacy. Founded in 2012, Tinybeans allows you to share your baby's milestones within a closed social network, accessible only to people you invite. They have amassed three million users, and Forbes reports they are growing at 2500 new users each day.[1]

Gen Z are experienced shoppers

Generation Z are incredibly comfortable with online shopping, but don't expect them to use a desktop to shop with you; mobile is the only way they will transact. Asia really leads the way in ecommerce. They are far more likely to shop online for speed than any other region of the world. That being said, Gen Z expert David Willey, founder of marketing agency Growth Tank, advises that traditional bricks-and-mortar stores continue to play a key role in Gen Z's retail experiences. He noted that while Gen Z certainly conduct their product research online, they prefer to make their purchases in store. Willey argues brands must ensure they are catering to Gen Z's desire for both the online and offline to win their custom.

Gen Z mums are entrepreneurial

Generation Z mothers will have more of an entrepreneurial mind-set than generations before them.[2] In many developed countries – including Australia – mothers are entering business in record numbers, and I expect this growth to be accelerated as Generation Z women become mothers. This is supported by US research, which found that Generation Z is 55% more likely to want to start a business than Millennials. These figures should represent great opportunities for the professional services industry, with these women requiring business education, coaching services and administration support. I believe we will see sales distribution channels change and open up, with more mums selling to other mums in

1   www.forbes.com/sites/meimeifox/2019/04/15/how-tinybeans-built-a-social-network-based-on-privacy/#4140a29f5e5d
2   www.forbes.com/sites/deeppatel/2017/09/21/8-ways-generation-z-will-differ-from-millennials-in-the-workplace/#16f20b0c76e5

their network. It will be different from the multi-level marketing that we see now.

Increasing mental health concerns

Generation Z spend more time on electronic media than in face-to-face interactions. Despite being more connected with their friends, there have been significant increases in mental health issues in this generation.[1] A UK study undertaken of 13,000 14 year olds by the Department of Education found increased rates of depression and anxiety, with 37% of girls feeling unhappy, worthless or unable to concentrate.[2] This was more than double the rate of boys. There are clearly opportunities for brands that can create products and services to better support Generation Z women as they become mothers.

Gen Z mums are purpose driven

These mothers are socially conscious. Your brand's purpose will be a critical element to your success. Your purpose will need to go far deeper than just being a marketing strategy; it will need to permeate your organisation.

To understand more about the growing importance of purpose, I reached out to Jeff Fromm, author of *The Purpose Advantage* and three other books, who said:

> *'Brand purpose drives consumer preference and price elasticity with values-driven Gen Z consumers as well as people with a youth mindset.'*

A recent VICE APAC study identified that three in four Generation Z consumers want to buy from brands that align with their values, while another study found that 69% of Generation Z

---

1 www.theguardian.com/lifeandstyle/2016/dec/10/generation-z-latest-data-teens
2 assets.publishing.service.gov.uk/government/uploads/system/uploads/attachment_data/file/599871/LSYPE2_w2-research_report.pdf

consumers will buy from companies that give money to and support good causes.[1] Be careful of 'green washing' though; Generation Z can sniff out inauthentic attempts to appear purpose driven in an instant, and the impact can be devastating to your bottom line.

Stacey Hicks, Editor and Content Director at *Girlfriend*, said:

'If I could give one piece of advice to brands wanting to reach Gen Z, it's to be authentic. These women are bombarded with messaging and they're more brand savvy than any generation before them, so it takes an honest and authentic moment of truth to really cut through. These women are willing to pay more for brands that align with their beliefs or stand for something.'

This generation of mothers will demand more from brands than we have seen before. They want brands to not only stand for something important to them, they also want brands to go a step further and make a difference. What difference is your brand going to make to their world?

The environment is very high on their list of concerns. The 2019 Junkee Media report shows there has been a significant increase in concern for the environment over the past six years. They are deeply concerned about the lack of environmental care shown by companies. Top of their environmental concerns is the climate.[2] They see this as an emergency, and want brands to be demonstrating how they are supporting the environment. This is likely to be heightened as they become parents and become more invested in creating a better world for their children.

---

1 www.smashingmagazine.com/2019/03/mobile-designers-generation-gen-z/
2 www.bandt.com.au/media/junkee-oohmedia-unveil-gender-change-research-project?utm_source=Adestra&utm_medium=email&utm_term=&utm_content=Junkee%20And%20oOh%21media%20Unveil%20A%20Gender%20For%20Change%20Research%20Project&utm_campaign=B%26T%20today%3A%207th%20June%202019

Transparency is key

Generation Z wants transparency, and the desire for brands to 'be real' will only be heightened with Gen Z mothers. They want to know what goes on behind the scenes. They want to know where their clothes are being made and under what conditions. They want to know how you treat your employees and suppliers. All of this counts for this upcoming generation of mothers.

Consider your imagery also. This generation of mothers wants images captured 'as you are'. They are not like Millennials seeking the perfect shot. They are comfortable in their own skin. Forget retouching your images; this generation of mums will trust and give their money to companies that use real people and customers in their advertising.

One Australian brand that is well positioned to cater for the Generation Z mother is Thank You, a social enterprise committed to ending global poverty. They produce products in the water, baby care, personal care and nappy categories. On the back of each of their products is an individual code. Purchasers can enter their unique code into the Thank You website and it allows the purchaser to track their impact. Not only does this help to connect the purchaser to the difference they are making, it allows Thank You to demonstrate their commitment of giving 100% of their profits to fund life-changing projects around the world. At the time of writing this book, Thank You had committed to helping 556,300 people with water, sanitation and hygiene projects.

Transparency is a key success factor across the globe. I reached out to Dino Jaegle, Co-Founder, WeMoms from France. WeMoms is an award-winning app for mothers where they can seek out parenting advice from a collection of other mothers and more than 500 parenting experts. WeMoms sees more than 150,000 experiences shared by French mothers every day. Dino believes:

'You can't consider mothers who have access to immediate and constant flows of information believe messages that are not correlated with truth. I believe that transparency and the capacity for brands to recognise their faults and errors, to assume that they are human and imperfect, will win.'

Gen Z are collaborative

Generation Z want to collaborate with brands. The US National Retail Federation reported that 44% of Gen Z consumers would be happy to share their ideas for product design.[1] We have seen this as a growing trend among mothers we've interviewed over the past five years; they increasingly want to be involved in new product development. This will be heightened over the next decade as Generation Z mothers become the core segment of the mum market. Savvy brands that adopt a collaborative new product development strategy will reap rewards.

Gen Z mums are risk averse

This generation of mothers will not have the same appetite for risk as Millennial mums. They are less experimental and not drinking, smoking or engaging in other risky pursuits as early as past generations. This aversion to risk is seen in their purchasing behaviours also. Third-party proof and endorsements by other mothers will be important in swaying their purchase decisions. Earned media will become more valuable as this generation becomes mothers, as they want to minimise their risk of purchase.

Gen Z mums are savers

Gen Z mothers will demonstrate a very different relationship with money and spending than Millennials. I spoke with Gen Z expert David Willey, the founder of Growth Tank, who has worked as

---

1 www.smashingmagazine.com/2019/03/mobile-designers-generation-gen-z/

a youth marketer for the past 15 years, working with a range of brands including Apple, Spotify and Google. David shared a study conducted by his Australian marketing agency, Growth Tank, which found that 57% of Gen Zs said they would rather save money than spend it immediately. David advises:

> *'They'll find the best deals and will expect to test out products physically or virtually before they buy. While this careful mindset presents more challenges for marketers, brands can reach these smart consumers by proving they are a reliable brand. Gen Zs will want brands to show their long-term value and make them feel safe. Instilling confidence in this generation can help brands gain loyal fans for life.'*

Safety focus

Generation Z exhibits a stronger focus on safety than previous generations. They have grown up in an age of terrorism and gun violence, particularly in the US. In the US, 95% of public schools run live shooter lockdown drills.[1] This need for safety will be heightened once they become parents. Demonstrating the safety aspects of your brand's offering will be an important success factor.

Stronger family influence

Generation Z listen to their elders. In fact, they enjoy spending time with their parents. It marks a significant change from Millennials who prefer to find their own way; Generation Z mothers are likely to seek advice from their mothers and grandmothers. Consequently, we will see a growing influence of grandmothers in coming years. If you don't have a strategy that includes grandma yet, it's time to start thinking about one.

---

1 https://www.theatlantic.com/magazine/archive/2019/03/active-shooter-drills-erika-christakis/580426/

Happiness and spirituality

While increasing numbers of this generation are not aligned with traditional religion, they do seek out the spiritual meaning in life. Stephanie Winkler, Head of Research and Insights at VICE Asia-Pacific, shared a recent study of Gen Z at the Youth Marketing Australia conference in Melbourne in May 2019, and reported that 8 in 10 Generation Zers surveyed do not partake in organised religion, and that 7 in 10 are on the quest for spirituality. She went on to share that 50% of people are looking for brands that will enhance their spirit and soul.

Success for Gen Z is judged upon feelings of happiness rather than wealth. Being happy is the measure of a good life. Right now, they get their great happiness from spending time with their friends, but I expect this will change significantly once they become parents. They are likely to prioritise enjoying fun things with their children. It will also be critical for brands to consider how they can provide a role in helping this generation of mothers reconnect with themselves as women post the birth of their children.

Gamifying

While gaming is far more popular among Gen Z males, females are also participating. Sean Callanan, Founder of Sports Geek in Australia and a big player in the esports space, says that males dominate the esports space, accounting for 88% of the audience, however women are enjoying esports also. And given it's the fastest growing sports segment in the world, it should be given some consideration. Smart marketers are adapting their marketing to include gaming mechanics, such as building quizzes and competitions into their awareness stage.

Diversity is the norm

Generation Z value diversity and inclusion more than any other generation. While Generation X and Millennial mothers have warmly received isolated brands' use of diverse models in their advertising, this will be an expectation of Gen Z.

This will be a generation of very different family structures, in all sorts of ways. Not only will we continue to see strong increases in interracial relationships, I anticipate many women will actively choose to become a solo parent through donor insemination or adoption. Realistically depicting different family structures in marketing communications will be critical to success over the next decade.

IRL

'In real life' (IRL) experiences are still important for Generation Z. Don't be fooled that it is *all* digital. Generation Z mothers and their partners will be seeking out unique experiences that support them, are aligned with their values, and help them achieve a sense of happiness.

Brand considerations

There are communication preferences for this upcoming segment of mothers that you will need to adapt your marketing strategy to accommodate. My key tips are:

- Generation Z love visual communications.

- Video is particularly important to this generation as they are not readers.

- Given their need for speed, it's imperative that your web copy doesn't waste their time.

- They want to co-create with brands.

- They want to be able to customise your offering.

- They are very entertainment driven. Whereas your brand might connect with other generations of mothers through emotive copy and imagery, Generation Z want to be attracted by your entertainment offering first.

- They value their privacy.
- They favour Instagram, YouTube and Snapchat.
- To be successful with this cohort of mothers you'll need to create something really special to facilitate word-of-mouth buzz among parents.

Opportunity #5: Mum-led businesses

Mums in business are an untapped, growing segment among the professional services market which many brands are overlooking. For the past decade, women in Australia have been entering business at almost three times the rate of men. These numbers are driven by women who are seeking more flexible working conditions and more meaningful work after the birth of a child. There are more than 300,000 mum-led businesses operating in Australia, powering the small business segment.

The rise of mum-led businesses is significant as it has resulted in a shift and expansion in the purchasing power of women. These women are excellent listeners, have superior problem-solving skills, and have a deep empathy that places them in the winning position to understand the problem they wish to solve in business. Their spend and influence is undeniable.

These mothers are purchasing a diverse range of products and services. They are engaging accounting, legal, insurance and advertising services. They are signing commercial leases and financing cars. Yet, despite the incredible breadth and influence of their spending, few brands are tapping into this growing market segment. If your brand caters to the small business market, have you allocated your marketing budget accordingly?

Mums & Co, a leading business mums' network in Australia, released an in-depth report in 2018 into the 'mums in business' category. The Mums & Co 'Australian Mums in Business' report was undertaken by EY Sweeney with 852 mums who either own a business or are considering starting a business.[1] The report revealed that the average mum in business is aged in her 30s with two children, and she's likely to be tertiary qualified. One-third of mum-led businesses were started while on parental leave, and six out of ten mums who started their businesses that year had an infant or toddler. An interesting finding in the report was that more than half of the respondents had started businesses in a completely new field to what they were doing before. This often means they are seeking adequately priced expert consulting support in an array of areas, including marketing, social media, administration, finance and legal.

It's a similar story across the globe. According to a 2018 study by SCORE Association in the US, women-owned businesses increased five times faster than the national average and comprise 39% of small businesses, generating more than US$1.6 trillion in revenue.[2] Interestingly, the majority of start-ups launching in the US are by women of colour, including African Americans, Latinas and Asian Americans.

The mothers of invention

Innovation is one of the key drivers of brand growth, and mums are emerging as masters of innovation. According to IP Australia, the number of women inventors in Australia grew tenfold over the past 30 years. Many of these patent holders are entrepreneurial mothers looking to solve problems after the birth of a child. These inventions are transforming the way we live, work and interact with the world.[3]

---

1   mumsandco.com.au/insight/what-inspired-the-australian-mums-in-business-repo
2   www.success.com/how-women-are-rising-in-business/
3   www.ipaustralia.gov.au/about-us/news-and-community/news/australia-closing-gender-gap-female-inventors

For example, Jennifer Holland launched Throat Scope in 2009 after a traumatic trip to the doctor with her young son. Asked to restrain her wriggling 15-month-old boy while the doctor inserted a wooden tongue depressor for an oral cavity examination, Jennifer thought there had to be a better way, and she started designing a new tool to do the job. One year later Jennifer won an innovation award from the Queensland Government, and then three years later secured a key investor after featuring on *Shark Tank*. Throat Scope launched into the Australian market in late 2015 with much excitement. Growth has been quick, and by the end of 2016 Throat Scope was available in almost 150 countries. Jennifer has picked up many awards, and her invention has become the most used screening tool to detect early signs of oral cancer. What an incredible invention, which originated from taking her sick child to the doctor.

Emma Lovell started CoziGo (formerly known as Fly Babee) after a year of constant long-distance travel with her first baby. Emma's mum was living in the UK and had been diagnosed with cancer, and Emma immediately relocated. But she found herself making frequent trips back to Australia so Emma's daughter could see her dad. With each trip, Emma arrived wrecked as her baby daughter had failed to sleep during the flight. Emma took to carrying around a spare sheet on flights so she could cover the bassinet, to help settle her daughter. Realising that other parents must be experiencing the same problem, Emma looked for a solution. This led to the creation of CoziGo, a black mesh cover that fits on top of a bassinet or pusher to block out light, assisting babies and toddlers to get to sleep. Emma gained great exposure on *Shark Tank* and secured funding and support from another mum, well-known Australian entrepreneur Janine Allis. The CoziGo is now used by parents as a sleep tool for both flying and also in the pram.

Australian mum of four Kristy Chong is the founder of Modibodi, which offers modern protective apparel for women designed to give them confidence and comfort. Modibodi provides a more sustainable solution to disposable hygiene. Kristy started the business in 2014 after experiencing some pelvic floor issues while training for a marathon after the birth of her second child. She spent the next 18 months developing her patent-protected technology before launching her online business. To date, Modibodi have sold one million pairs globally.

Kristy found success via public relations, social media and the use of influencers in helping to build trust with consumers. Kristy found that mainstream Australian retailers were very cautious in their ranging decisions, particularly when it came to an innovative product dealing with largely taboo topics of bladder leakage, menstruation, discharge and perspiration.

Kristy believes the key to Modibodi's success is a mix of having a unique product, strong, strategic and engaging marketing and social media, as well as direct communications with customers. She believes it's been important to have a mix of activities to ensure her brand can reach as many prospective customers as possible.

Modibodi has four localised ecommerce sites in Australia, the US, Europe and the UK, as well as being on the Amazon Marketplace in the US as she sets her sights on creating a global, sustainable business.

Modibodi's Give a Pair Program aims to provide homeless women in Modibodi underwear that is sustainable and reusable to empower these women at the times they need it. For every 'virtual pair' voucher purchased, Modibodi donate two pairs of physical underwear to women's shelters and women in need across Australia throughout the year.

It's a similar story across the world.

Brand considerations

As someone who has mentored and supported more than 100 mum-led businesses in the past five years, the key challenges I've seen are around money, mindset and marketing. Many struggle to adequately finance their business. Hence, there exists an opportunity for brands within the financial services area to assist mothers to find access to information about different ways to finance and grow their business. Can you advise on grants, accelerators, or capital equity options for mum-led businesses? Can you help them better understand their numbers and teach them how to read financial statements? There are strong growth opportunities in educating and supporting these women on their business journeys.

Confidence is also an area of concern. Many of the mums I've mentored feel isolated, and struggle with gaining the confidence to think big and push themselves well outside their comfort zone. This provides opportunities for service-based businesses in the areas of:

- mindset
- goal setting
- business strategy and planning
- business accelerators
- co-working environments that have childcare facilities.

Business events that allow these mums to upskill and meet other mum business owners are also important as the micro entrepreneurs (those who employ fewer than four people) are often working from home and feel isolated.

However, perhaps the greatest pain point I have found among this market segment is around marketing. How can they attract customers to their business on a limited budget? Answering this very question led me to write my first book *Marketing to Mums*. The majority of book sales have originated from mum business owners who are also looking to attract mothers to their business. They were attracted to the simple eight-step framework of things they can implement into their business at low cost.

The growth in mum-led businesses is set to continue. In fact, I believe we will see significant changes over the next decade as investors start to realise the profit opportunities available to them by backing women entrepreneurs. The increasing support of women in the start-up sector across the globe – fuelled by the likes of Springboard Enterprises – will see women-led businesses grow and prosper.

This view is shared by Jola Burnett, Vice President at GfK:

> *'The time to innovate for moms has never been better. There are opportunities to design products and services with functionalities that truly respond to the underserved moms' needs. Creating new products and services with the pragmatic mom in mind is key to building meaningful connections and repeat business. I also see an opportunity to engage female engineers, coders and investors for leading roles in the digital revolution, product design and innovation.'*

And Bec Brideson, a Creative Agency owner, has recently launched Women with Agency, which is looking to implement gender fair procurement reform:

> *'Currently 1% of global procurement contracts go to women-owned businesses ... Women with Agency is ensuring that women-owned businesses can truly compete in a meritocracy. In the same way that progressive companies recruit 50/50 without gender bias, let's see pitch procurement policy catch up too.'*[1]

How can *your* brand create specific service offerings that support and address their notable pain points?

---

1   https://womenwithagency.com/

Opportunity #6: Migrant mums

National identities are changing, yet I feel brands haven't caught up. Migrant mums – those not born in the country in which they reside – represent a largely untapped opportunity. They are a compelling and overlooked market. In Australia, 29% of residents (more than seven million people) were born in another country, the most common origins being England, China and India.[1] It's not surprising then that the number of people who speak Chinese languages at home in Australia has increased 400% since 1986.[2]

In Canada, 21% of residents (representing almost seven million people) were born in another country.[3] Asian-born Canadians represent 57% of immigrants, with the Philippines being the most common country of origin, followed by China and India.

This represents a significant shift from the 1970s, when the majority of migrants to these countries came from Europe.

In Germany, 15% of the population was born in another country. Migrant women from Romania, Bulgaria and Syria are driving Germany's birth rate; one in four children born in 2016 was to a migrant mother. The high rate is the result of Germany's assistance to Eastern Europeans seeking asylum.

In the US, 14% of residents (representing around 46 million people) were born in another country.[4] While Mexicans represent 25% of all US migrants, there is a growing opportunity among Asian Americans, with Pew Research reporting that the Asian American population almost doubled between 2000 and 2015.[5] Asian Americans are highly educated, likely to live in multi-generational households, and favour living on the west coast

1   www.businessinsider.com.au/australia-population-immigration-2018-2019-4
2   www.facebook.com/absstats/photos/a.422649347796410/2324272424300750/?type=3&theater
3   www12.statcan.gc.ca/nhs-enm/2011/as-sa/99-010-x/99-010-x2011001-eng.cfm
4   www.migrationpolicy.org/article/frequently-requested-statistics-immigrants-and-immigration-united-states
5   www.pewresearch.org/fact-tank/2017/09/08/key-facts-about-asian-americans/

of America, with California being a particularly popular location. Nielsen reports that Asian Americans' buying power is expected to rise to US$1.3 trillion by 2022, making them a lucrative market segment.[1] In these four countries alone, we are talking about a market of more than 350 million people, with mums being the gateway into the family purchasing. Yet multicultural communities are going largely unnoticed. A UK report claims 77% of British Asians feel that mainstream advertising has little relevance to them.[2]

Migrants are usually very comfortable purchasing online and are very tech focused. They tend to reside in urban areas where it is easier for them to find work.

Higher fertility rates

Migrant mums are reducing the impact of declining birth rates. In the US, migrants represent 14% of the population, however they represent 23% of all births.[3] This trend is echoed in Australia, with migrant women fertility rates doubling non-migrant women. They also bring a rich tapestry of diversity to their new countries.

Strong – and increasing – buying power

The multicultural community has strong buying power that should not be underestimated. In the UK, the multicultural population has over £300 billion in disposable income.[4] In the US, *Inc.* magazine reports that their buying power increased at double the pace of the entire country, to be valued at US$3.4 trillion in 2014.[5] These figures cannot be ignored, and provide real growth opportunities for brands willing to invest resources into deeply understanding

1 www.nielsen.com/us/en/insights/reports/2018/asian-americans-consumers.html
2 gottabemarketing.co.uk/why-invest-in-ethnicmarketing/
3 www.pewresearch.org/fact-tank/2017/08/29/over-the-past-25-years-immigrant-moms-bolstered-births-in-48-states/
4 gottabemarketing.co.uk/why-invest-in-ethnicmarketing/
5 www.inc.com/yuriy-boykiv/multicultural-marketing-no-longer-an-option-but-a-necessity.html

key ethnicities and cultural heritage. Mothers are the gateway into these families.

Migrant social media communities

Migrant mothers tend to be more active in social media communities. Often living in countries without their own family, they seek out new friendships with others who understand their cultural backgrounds, customs and traditions. It can assist them to overcome any feelings of culture shock, as they start to assimilate into their new country but wish to hold onto their culture and heritage. In the US, Latinos have significantly higher use of social media compared to other ethnicities, and they are also more inclined to engage in online shopping from their mobile phone. In Australia, migrant mothers come together across more than 100 Facebook groups. These groups are very active, with Indian Mums Connect – which has more than 20,000 members – being one of the most popular.[1] Many of these online friendships develop into life-long offline friendships with other families from their country of origin. They act as a family away from their home country. They support each other, and share tips about brands to support and those to avoid.[2]

Having a high use of Facebook and often sending money back to family members in their country of origin, it's likely that Libra – Facebook's cryptocurrency offering – will be very well received by migrant mothers. I will be watching with great interest as I believe uptake within this segment will be over-indexed. Facebook has reported that transaction fees associated with these international transfers add up to US$25 billion each year.[3]

---

1 www.broadagenda.com.au/home/digital-commuity-mothering-how-migrant-mothers-in-australia-build-community-on-facebook/
2 mashable.com/2015/07/24/multicultural-marketing-tactics/
3 newsroom.fb.com/news/2019/06/coming-in-2020-calibra/

Chinese and Indian migrant mothers

Globally there are significant numbers of Chinese and Indian migrants who have resettled abroad. They represent an emerging market for brands, particularly those that are looking to achieve growth via exporting to China and India. These people represent a great opportunity to promote products to migrant mothers *before* exporting to their country of origin. For example, as part of an entry into China, brands might promote their products or services to Chinese migrant mothers in their home country, stimulating word-of-mouth recommendations to their friends and relatives back in China and India, effectively acting as influencers.

This should be an important part of any brand's China or India go-to-market strategy. Communicate with them via their preferred social media platforms of WeChat and, for younger mothers, Weibo.

Cultural events

Brands also have opportunities to engage with migrant mothers via key cultural moments. For example, both the US and Australia have a high number of Chinese migrant mothers, so creating a campaign to celebrate Chinese New Year would be worth considering.

In doing so, it's important that your brand's attempt doesn't appear tokenistic. Take the time to really understand migrant mums the meaning of the cultural event. This can only be achieved by taking the time to understand their heritage and eagerness to become part of their new country. Make sure you avoid stereotypes and clichés. Those who achieve cut-through do things differently.

Culturally diverse workforces

If you are looking for growth, it would be remiss of me not to mention the opportunity to employ migrant mothers. Often highly educated and with extensive skills and experience, they can add rich perspective to your work teams and provide representation of your consumers. Don't underestimate the value of having a diverse workforce. I spoke with cultural intelligence expert Anoushka Gungadin, CEO of Global CQ:

> 'In today's globalised world, the risk for business lies in not embracing inclusion as part of growth strategy. There is a shift in consumer expectations from the industrial leadership style of the Baby Boomers to an inclusive and egalitarian leadership style for Millennials. The workplace needs to be reflective of the marketplace and, by extension, society. In fact, the diversity dividend includes increases in innovation, creativity, engagement and financial bottom line.'

There is a clear correlation between a diverse workforce and financial performance.[1] A 2015 McKinsey report found that companies that are culturally diverse at an executive level were 33% more likely to deliver profits considered above average.[2] Migrant mothers will add to your financial performance.

Brand considerations

Success hinges on keeping pace with increasingly diverse populations and understanding their core needs. You need to deeply understand their culture in order to appeal to them. Empathy is required, so it's important that you don't make assumptions.

I spoke with Mita Mallick who heads up Cross Cultural Marketing at Unilever North America, to better understand cross-cultural marketing considerations for brands. Mita has achieved enormous success within Unilever on their journey to remove cultural bias throughout their marketing teams. She has co-created the first-of-its-kind Cultural Immersions series to increase the cultural competency of marketers, training over 3000

---

1   www.forbes.com/sites/karstenstrauss/2018/01/25/more-evidence-that-company-diversity-leads-to-better-profits/#2dea459e1bc7

2   www.mckinsey.com/business-functions/organization/our-insights/why-diversity-matters

marketers to date. Mita recommends that brands wanting to appeal to migrant mothers should:

'Avoid stereotyping mothers. Deeply understand who you are serving. Understand their lived experience as a mother. You can start with the insight that as mothers we all want the best for our children and families. And how mothers express care and love can show up differently depending on the culture. If as marketers we also happen to be mothers, we have to be careful not to insert our own bias and cultural lens on what mothers want and need.'

Opportunity #7: Pregnant women and first-time mums

Getting pregnant and having your first baby is a major life event. Pregnancy is a time of deep research, preparation and excitement. Becoming a parent sees women on a steep learning curve as they become more familiar with sleep deprivation and the responsibilities associated with raising a child. It represents a significant transition for many people as their identity shifts from individual to parent.

A valuable audience for businesses

Pregnant women and first-time mothers represent a highly desired audience.[1] Brands want to start their relationships with expectant mothers and join them throughout parenthood. Forbes estimates the value of first-time Milllennial mothers to be US$46 billion in the US alone.[2] And this figure is only set to increase. These women expect brands to invest time in getting to know them prior to

---

1   www.zahramediagroup.com/marketing-to-pregnant-women/
2   www.forbes.com/sites/tanyaklich/2019/05/10/the-new-mom-economy-meet-the-startups-disrupting-the-46-billion-millennial-parenting-market/#1ba34aab5130

selling, something they feel is not being adequately addressed by brands, and herein lies the opportunity.

Becoming a parent is an expensive milestone. In the UK, expectant parents spend £1600 during pregnancy, while first-time parents are estimated to add £500m to the economy each year.[1] First-time mothers account for 40% of births in Ireland and the US. A Choice study says parents in Australia are likely to spend up to $13,000 on a child during their first year.[2] To put this into perspective, let's talk nappies. Choice estimates a child is likely to use 6000 nappies before being toilet trained, making them incredibly attractive to nappy brands.[3]

First-time mothers also influence the purchasing behaviours of other mothers. As a woman becomes a mother, research reveals that they are eight times more likely to talk about brands than before they had children.[4] This effectively sees first-time mothers becoming a marketing channel themselves. It's imperative that brands are working hard to provide mums with exceptional experiences at all points along the path to purchase and beyond, so they can have mums advocating for them.

Delayed motherhood

In Australia, we've seen a rapid increase in mothers giving birth in their 30s and 40s. The Australian Bureau of Statistics reveals that birth rates have doubled for women aged 35 to 39 and tripled for women aged 40 to 44 since 1987.[5] It's a similar story across the developed countries of the world, with the average age of

1   digitalmarketingmagazine.co.uk/articles/do-brands-really-get-what-matters-to-new-mums/3532
2   www.babycenter.com.au/a559811/buying-for-baby-on-a-budget
3   www.choice.com.au/babies-and-kids/baby-clothes-and-nappies/nappies/buying-guides/disposable-and-cloth-nappies
4   fleishmanhillard.com/2019/05/brand-marketing/marketing-to-mom-at-mothers-day/
5   www.perthnow.com.au/news/nsw/teen-birth-rate-drops-as-women-wait-to-have-kids-ng-d7394e1b07a5c51c5fec12e17af8381a?fbclid=IwAR0n-z2EFAsk1kwEM8QgLJsJb4XZEm yFBl0jDaSUpIOZs9J7vOE1rpUbr54

first-time mothers increasing. Today the average age of a first-time mum ranges from 18 years in many African countries through to 31 years of age in Greece and Australia. Most developed countries are somewhere between 26 and 31 years of age, so we are talking about Millennial mothers. Given the delay in parenthood, these Millennial mothers are now the most educated we've ever seen. They have established careers and are financially independent. These mothers (and fathers) take parenting very seriously. Safety is one of their top concerns. They rely on testimonials to assist them with purchase decisions, and will research extensively, more so than previous generations. Research also shows Millennial mothers are more likely to try to do things to ensure their child gets ahead (much more than previous generations).[1] This is perhaps related to their own high education levels.

Feeling stressed and unsupported

Motherly, a US website for mums which boasts 30 million-plus monthly unique users, conducted a robust survey of 6457 Millennial mothers in March and April 2019.[2] Their 'State of Motherhood' report reveals 85% of mothers believe society does not do a good job of understanding and supporting mothers. Clearly there is work to be done, as this figure was up from 74% the previous year. The report paints a picture of a stressed and unsupported mother, with 51% of mothers feeling discouraged about combining career and motherhood, citing that they find it extremely challenging managing the trade-offs. Despite the majority returning to work after the birth of a child, 61% report doing the bulk of the household chores, with only 32% saying they were shared equally. In fact, mothers are more likely to spend more time on chores than they

---

1 blog.pregnancymagazine.com/study-of-new-attitudes-to-motherhood-can-help-in-marketing-to-moms/
2 s3.amazonaws.com/roar-assets-auto.rbl.ms/documents/2320/Motherly%202019%20State%20of%20Motherhood%20Survey%20Tables%20-%20Cleaned%20and%20Weighted%20-%20Millennial%20Only%2020190416.pdf

do on themselves. When asked where they feel they need the most support, the top response was to support their physical and mental health.

The Motherly report shows that while Millennials might consciously enter parenthood on equal terms, once the baby arrives practicalities are taking over, and mothers continue to pick up the bulk of household work and childcare. Employers need to think about how they can better support mothers as they transition back to work, and support fathers so they can take on greater domestic responsibilities also. There are many opportunities here for new products and services. One business that demonstrates a deep understanding of nursing mothers and supporting them is Milk Stork, the world's first breast milk shipping company helping professional women to get their breast milk back home while they are travelling. The company was launched in the US in 2015 by working mum Kate Torgersen, who struggled to maintain her breastfeeding of twins after she returned to work. She made it her mission to support other working mums to continue to breastfeed after returning to work. This is a major problem to solve, with research showing 25% of US women return to work within two weeks of giving birth, largely as a result of the absence of maternity leave.[1] Milk Stork has been embraced by mothers and employers. I first heard about it when I was interviewing Mita Mallick – Head of Diversity at Unilever North America – to discuss engaging mothers in the workplace. Milk Stork is supporting 15,000 travelling mothers in the US, and they've successfully partnered with more than 500 companies to help them retain great female talent. In 2019 they announced their service would expand to support mothers travelling internationally.

---

1   www.vox.com/2015/8/21/9188343/maternity-leave-united-states

I spoke with Kate about Milk Stork's success:

'Milk Stork is successful because it provides an elegant solution to an acute and recurring pain point that so many working moms have faced for years – pumping on business trips. We are also successful because working, breastfeeding moms are advocating for greater support in the workplace and asking their employers to support them with Milk Stork.'

Mums are calling out for more brands and business ideas which can better support them. By delving deeply into understanding this group of women, new opportunities will emerge. Women will tell you what they want.

Their values

According to the Motherly 'State of Motherhood' report, kindness is the most desired quality mothers want to instil in their children.[1] This is most pronounced among Caucasian mothers, with Hispanic and African-American mothers wanting to teach their children respect and resilience also. This is critical information considering that mothers are looking to purchase from brands that are aligned with their beliefs and values.

Internet use

Pregnant women will consume significantly more blogs and articles as they research what they need to know about becoming a parent. In fact, a Google consumer survey found that new and expectant mothers performed twice as many online searches as non-parents. Their smartphone was the primary device used to search the internet, with new and expectant parents being 2.7 times more likely than non-parents to use a smartphone as their primary search

---

1   www.mother.ly/2019-state-of-motherhood-survey

device.[1] The younger the parent, the more internet searching they engage in.

Social media use

Social media use increases once women become mothers. They post more photos also.[2] The primary choice of social media platform depends greatly on their location, but Facebook is particularly strong in Australia, the US, Singapore, Thailand and India, while WeChat dominates in China.

Social media is critical for brands for:

- building rapport
- sharing testimonials from other parents
- developing trust
- demonstrating your superior customer experience.

Social media should be used to share your brand story and focus on communicating your brand values and points of difference. Focus heavily on emotive storytelling via social media when connecting with mothers.

Trends

I sought out Phillip Lynch from Johnson & Johnson to learn more about key trends and growth opportunities within the baby category. As the former Vice President Baby Products for Asia and current Vice President of Commercial Growth and Innovation for Asia Pacific at Johnson & Johnson, his insights are incredibly valuable for brands:

'The boom in baby skincare natural and organic entries, particularly from niche brands, reflects mums' increasing

---

1   www.thinkwithgoogle.com/consumer-insights/new-parents/
2   blog.globalwebindex.com/marketing/cpg-brands-us-chinese-mothers-2019/

view that natural is better, and that small and new brands are assumed to be better than well-established legacy brands.

'Transparency is a hallmark for what the mother of today expects from business. That means brands need to be transparent on where products are manufactured, how ingredients are sourced and, for some brands whose positioning is purpose based, how they interact with stakeholders in a unique and relevant manner.

'Direct-to-consumer is growing rapidly, and businesses large and small are watching its development to ensure they can capitalise accordingly. Direct relationship affords unique opportunities for consumer and shopper insights, relationships and value creation, particularly for the high-engagement baby products business.'

Purchase behaviours

Setting up for a new baby involves many high-value purchases, including a cot and pram. Given the high spend, pregnant women and their partners will research extensively. They take to social media and are highly influenced by what other people are saying about products. According to a 2018 GlobalWebIndex study of more than 2000 Chinese and US mothers, quality is the number one purchase driver when appealing to new mothers, and they are willing to pay a premium for a higher quality product.[1] Quality ranks higher as a consideration when selling to first-time mothers versus existing mothers. Testimonials have primary influence on their spending decisions, as one of our Marketing to Mums 2019 survey participants pointed out:

'I find reviews the most helpful when researching a product or service for our baby. Hearing the pros and cons from people in

---

1   www.globalwebindex.com/hubfs/Downloads/Marketing-to-Moms-eBook.pdf

the same position as you is a big influencer for us. Incorporating reviews into each individual product you have on your site would absolutely increase my likelihood of making a purchase. Also, include links to your site from bigger review sites on the best reviewed items. So, when the decision is made, you know where to purchase.'

Understanding the pregnancy journey

It's critical that brands understand the pregnancy journey when trying to sell to pregnant women, from discovering you are pregnant, to the first scan, to finishing work and waiting for the arrival, to the birth, to the first car ride home. Successful brands understand the new-parent moments and milestones that can trigger information searching and purchasing. One of the key things to recognise is that pregnant women expecting their first child will start to purchase much earlier than expectant current mothers. They will start to look at purchasing at four or five months into their pregnancy. Understanding these timings is critical.

Connecting with other mums

New mothers want to connect with other mothers. They gravitate to platforms that enable them to do this, hence the popularity of closed Facebook groups and mum friendship app Peanut. They seek advice from other mums as they are in the early stages of their journey to parenthood, and they don't have the knowledge or confidence other mums with multiple children might have. This is their time of brand discovery. As a company, you might want to look at ways you can bring new mothers together, whether that be online or in person.

'Make things simple and easy to understand for first-time mums like me who get so overwhelmed. Sometimes products can be so confusing, and I'm not really sure they are necessary.

I get most of my advice regarding products from a Facebook group supporting pregnant women.'

Marketing to Mums survey (2019)

Developing a new identity as a mum

There is usually a period of transition that takes place up to around 18 months after birth in which first-time mothers are adjusting to their new identity as a mum. It's vitally important brands recognise that many mothers struggle with this transition. They need empathy, support and reassurance.

They also want brands to reflect their other interests. In our Marketing to Mums research we have repeatedly found that mothers want to be treated as women first, mothers second. They tell us that motherhood is incredibly important to them but it is not *all of them*, and they want to be reflected as the multi-dimensional women they are. Brands that box mum into just being mum or use stereotypical imagery and language will quickly fall out of favour. Showing a range of different family structures, ethnicities and a diversity of situations and abilities is important.

John Lewis ran a brilliant campaign in 2010 that focused on the women-first approach to marketing to mothers. The campaign showed the progression of a young girl through to an older grandparent to the soundtrack of *You're Always a Woman to Me*. It worked. It deeply resonated with mothers. Can your brand be adopting a woman-first approach to reaching new mothers?

Don't forget dad

Dads are far more active in Millennial and Generation Z households – we commonly see them enter parenthood on equal terms with mum. Dads are likely to be at all the medical appointments, scans and baby showers, but equally, you'll see them researching cots, pushers and visiting baby stores. So, consider that dad will also be using the nappy bag, pusher and baby carrier. Make sure he feels comfortable with the design too. In recent times, we've even seen the emergence of online platforms just for dads, to assist them through their journey as a father.

> *'I think brands stereotype mums and forget a growing trend of the stay-at-home dad. My wife earns more than me, so it makes sense for me to stay at home with the children. Being inclusive of mums and dads and understanding not every household fits the mainstream anymore would be a good start. Sometimes I feel left out of the conversation. I would be more inclined to purchase if it was inclusive.'*
>
> *Marketing to Mums survey (2019)*

And don't overlook your marketing communications also. A FanFinders survey of 5330 mothers in 2015 revealing that 87% of respondents felt brands should incorporate fathers more in marketing. It's a view shared by Phillip Lynch, Vice President of Commercial Growth and Innovation at Johnson & Johnson, Asia Pacific, who believes:

> *'Brands need to consider fathers, as mums are increasingly looking to them for support and partnering in parenting, so brands who integrate that view will be viewed more progressively.'*

Pampers have looked to acknowledge the greater involvement of dads at home, teaming up with John Legend to show a team of fathers caring for their babies. It uses fun, playful communications – John Legend sings a song about the need to change his baby's nappy. Mums like the commercial as it acknowledges that dads are stepping up at home, while dads like that they are being included in the brand communication. Further to this, they have announced they will install 5000 nappy change stations in male restrooms by 2021.[1] However, it's important to come back to the data. While dads are becoming more involved, they are still significantly less likely to be the primary carer for a child and subsequently are less likely to be the primary person responsible for household spend.[2] One recent report claimed fathers are only helping out by an extra seven minutes over the past 15 years.[3] This is unlikely to change until organisations actively encourage men to take parental leave. Brands do need to consider them, however it's important to recognise that mothers remain the key decision makers in the majority of households.

Baby tech explosion

The baby category is experiencing rapid growth as new Millennial parents purchase tools to assist them to manage their journey through parenthood. They are actively seeking out mobile solutions to their problems, and this has led to a baby tech boom. IBIS predicts that the baby product industry is set to grow significantly, reaching US$10.4 billion in revenue by 2023.[4] In Australia, the baby product category is defying tough retail conditions and generating double-digit growth. Venture capital firms are starting to see the enormous opportunity on offer in catering for first-time mothers. Forbes writer Tanya Klich reports that US$500 million has been invested in disruptive start-ups catering for new mothers up until Mother's Day 2019.[5]

For example, Owlet is an award-winning 'smart sock' and app which allows parents to track temperature, heart rate, oxygen levels and movement without waking their baby. The app allows you to

1   www.usatoday.com/story/money/business/2019/06/12/pampers-diaper-changing-stations-mens-restrooms/1429533001/
2   she-conomy.com/report/marketing-to-women-quick-facts
3   womensagenda.com.au/latest/the-global-report-on-fathers-that-ought-to-be-mandatory-reading/
4   www.inc.com/emily-canal/best-industries-2019-owlet.html
5   www.forbes.com/sites/tanyaklich/2019/05/10/the-new-mom-economy-meet-the-startups-disrupting-the-46-billion-millennial-parenting-market/#1ba34aab5130

pre-set levels, and alerts you if your baby stops breathing.[1] Owlet was founded by two American dads, and provides reassurance, peace of mind, reduced anxiety, and helps promote better sleep in parents so they are in better shape to meet the increasing demands and expectations of being a parent. An astounding 94% of parents using Owlet have reported sleeping better themselves and 96% have reported less anxiety. The product, appropriate for babies up to 18 months of age, sells for approximately US$299.

Owlet has proven incredibly popular among first-time mothers, and it has garnered a great deal of attention among the business community.[2] They've amassed a social community in excess of 860,000 mothers, and are tipped to turn over US$50 million this year, with Forbes listing them as one of the next billion-dollar companies.[3] However, the success of the business is not hinged on selling smart socks; the real value is in the data collected by Owlet. They have incredibly rich data about baby sleep patterns that is ripe for commercialising. They are now focusing their attention on pregnant women, developing a band that will monitor a foetal heartbeat between visits to the doctor, again focusing on giving pregnant women peace of mind.

Snoo is an award-winning 'smart bassinet' and app that mimics womb-like rocking and white noise to facilitate sleep among babies.[4] Snoo was developed by Dr Harvey Karp, a high-profile US paediatrician and child development expert who is also the author of *The Happiest Baby on the Block*. It serves to reduce exhaustion in new parents by boosting babies' sleep, soothing unsettled babies and keeping them safer by keeping them on their back. Snoo will respond to a baby's cries, and automatically works to settle the baby with gentle rocking, allowing tired parents to get extra, less

1 owletcare.com.au
2 www.inc.com/emily-canal/best-industries-2019-owlet.html
3 www.forbes.com/pictures/hjff45gdj/owlet/#77cb363e40f0
4 money.cnn.com/2017/08/10/technology/gadgets/snoo-review/index.html

disturbed sleep. The product has been embraced by new mums in the US, Australia and Canada, with excellent online reviews. Since launching in 2016, Snoo Smart Sleeper has received strong financial backing, completing Series A and B funding rounds and attracting financial support from many Hollywood A-list celebrity parents. Companies are now offering Snoo sleepers to parents as a company perk to help them be more rested, enabling them to make better decisions in the workplace.[1]

What mums are really searching

In 2016 I had the pleasure of hearing from Google's Human Truths Manager at the M2Moms® – The Marketing to Moms conference in New York. The role of the Human Truths Manager is to identify emerging behavioural shifts and deep human truths about people's search behaviour to illuminate opportunities for brands. They shared a study undertaken in 2015 across eight countries which looked at nine billion Google searches and more than 70 million parenting YouTube video views by both new and experienced mums with children aged up to two years. The outcome was three 'truths' of modern motherhood which provide deep insights for brands wishing to connect and build relationships with this lucrative group of women.

Modern motherhood truth #1

The research highlighted that mums across the world are struggling to make themselves feel together again after the birth of a child. Mums were struggling to traverse the new landscape which is motherhood, and regain a sense of who and what their body was prior to having a baby, 'post-pregnancy hair loss' being one of the most highly searched questions by mothers. Also, mums wanted to know how to cope with stretch marks and skin issues post birth.

---

1 www.mother.ly/news/you-can-now-rent-the-snoo

The opportunity here for marketers is to consider content or products that address these issues and focus on helping mums feel great about their body again. Google suggested a self-care kit for mums after having a baby might make an interesting addition to some product ranges.

Modern motherhood truth #2

The Google research revealed that mums learn from their babies. Mums become increasingly concerned with what products they put on their babies' skin, and in doing so, start to question what products they actually put on their own skin. Many research participants cited spending increasing amounts on better quality skincare, hair care and cosmetics for themselves after the arrival of a child. They also identified that they were now looking for more do-it-yourself style products for their beauty regime rather than attending a day spa, as they didn't get the opportunity to do this much anymore.

This highlights opportunities for content that shows some easy hacks of natural, self-care things mums can do at home.

Modern motherhood truth #3

Mums re-evaluate their connections with products and brands they use at home after the birth of a child. Not only is mum now concerned about the products she is placing on baby's skin, she is also looking at her home environment. There is a clear drive towards reducing chemicals, using fewer fragrances, and finding products that have safer packaging in the home. The top three things mums are re-evaluating are:

- laundry products
- cleaning products
- aerosols and sprays.

Google suggested developing content around simple cleaning products that can be made at home and don't use harmful chemicals.

Google's study can assist brands to gain a deeper understanding of mums and their 'real' concerns. It's evident that new mothers are searching for support and assistance to transition and navigate their new role as mothers. As marketers, this provides an excellent opportunity for us to demonstrate that we can support them, make them feel more positive about their bodies, and assist them to create a safe environment at home.

A word of caution

If you are an employer, you must address your internal policies for pregnant women and parents. If you don't want to lose them, you must understand what your female employees value on their return to work. This is a key time when women leave. Reasons include:

- the juggle of parenthood and a career being too difficult

- unrealistic work expectations forcing them into the gig economy as a freelancer

- launching their own business to deliver the flexibility they or the father need

- seeking more meaningful work.

I recently spoke with Mita Mallick, Head of Diversity and Cross Cultural Marketing at Unilever North America, about engaging new mothers in the workplace for the Marketing to Mums podcast. Six years ago, Unilever focused on their retention of parents and implemented a series of new policies. In late 2018 they were named the best place to work for US mothers by Working Mother Media. Mita believes that listening to the individual needs of each woman is key. Don't make assumptions about what they want or need. Ask them how you can best support them. In Mita's first year in her role she spent most of the year speaking to people within Unilever, listening to and understanding what they wanted. This led to a wave of new offerings to better support parents, which included:

- changes to parental leave

- supporting IVF and egg freezing

- offering feeding rooms

- offering Milk Stork services while travelling.

Employers have a real responsibility to make sure they are creating a work environment that takes account of the needs of parents.

Opportunity #8: Grandmothers

Whether we are talking about yayas in Greece, halmoni in Korea or bestemor in Norway, grandmothers are an emerging superpower for marketers. They are a large, affluent, diverse market segment, and they *love* to indulge their grandchildren.

Worldwide there are more than one billion grandparents.[1] In the UK, there are 14 million grandparents, while the US has more than 70 million grandparents.[2] New research from AARP reveals that grandparents in the US are responsible for spending US$179 billion per year on their grandchildren, an average of US$2562 per year.[3] By 2030 there will be more people of grandparent age than children, so their impact is only going to get stronger.[4]

In industrialised countries people become grandparents in their early 50s, while in developing countries the age is generally a bit younger.[5] In the US the average age of a first-time grandparent is 50, and this is expected to increase in coming years as women delay motherhood. If we were comparing this market with other

1   grandparenteffect.com/guess-how-many-grandparents
2   www.informationnow.org.uk/article/grandparent-issues
3   www.aarp.org/research/topics/life/info-2019/aarp-grandparenting-study.html
4   www.legacyproject.org/specialreports/fastfacts.html
5   considerable.com/first-time-grandparents-age

groupings, grandmothers represent an incredibly affluent market, yet many brands are yet to establish a clear strategy to engage them.

Modern grandmothers

I spoke with Patty David, Director of Customer Insights from AARP – a non-profit membership organisation in the US with 38 million members – to dispel some commonly held misconceptions. Patty confirmed that grandmothers today are youthful, fit, healthy, tech savvy, financially astute, travel focused and extremely misrepresented by brands:

> 'Most Hallmark cards picture "grandma" as an older person with gray hair setting in a rocking chair knitting, but that is not the modern grandmother. The modern grandmother is on the go, still in the workforce, physically active, and engaging with grandchildren through technology. Picture a rollercoaster versus a rocking chair!
>
> 'Grandmothers play an increasingly important role in the family. They are the source of wisdom, legacy and storytelling. They are comfortable giving advice and talking to their grandchildren about morals and values, social etiquette, and college and career plans. Grandmothers are accepting of differences and encourage their grandchildren to know about their heritage.'

Grandmothers are embracing technology. Don't be surprised to find grandmothers setting up a Snapchat or Instagram account to communicate with their grandchildren. They love nothing more than to text their grandchildren using an array of hilarious emojis in their quest to stay current and relevant with their grandkids. A UK report commissioned by Disney on Ice in 2018 revealed that 75% of grandparents learn how to use technology from their grandchildren.[1] This might include setting up their smartphone, streaming music or setting up on-demand TV such as Netflix.

In the US, Pew Research from 2014 reports that 65% of women over 65 use social networking sites, with Facebook being their platform of choice, and Facebook Lives are also popular.[2,3] AARP reports that grandparents don't favour books and newspapers. In fact, they want to receive their information electronically, from the internet and email. Technology skills increased in importance when grandparents didn't live in the same location as their grandchildren, which is common.[4]

YouTube is also growing in popularity among grandmothers. A 'Think With Google' study found that Baby Boomers are more likely to watch a YouTube tutorial to learn how to do something over reading instructions, while one in three use YouTube to learn about a product or service.[5] YouTube is a format brands should be considering to connect and engage with grandmothers.

A Startsat60.com survey of people over 60 in Australia revealed that 94% of them researched online before a significant purchase.[6] They favour a softly-softly approach to selling, saying they respond best to being educated about a product or service first. Avoid the hard sell at all costs; they will respond well to storytelling elements.

The joy of being a grandparent

Being a grandparent delivers immense joy and keeps them youthful. One study shows that 72% think being a grandparent is the single most important and satisfying thing in their lives.[7] They see their

1   www.independent.co.uk/news/uk/home-news/grandparents-technology-grandchildren-learning-social-media-a8520731.html
2   www.pewinternet.org/2014/04/03/appendix-detailed-demographic-tables/
3   melmagazine.com/en-us/story/the-unsung-tech-savvy-of-grandmothers
4   marketingtomums.com.au/podcast/ep15_patty_david_grandparents_influence/
5   www.thinkwithgoogle.com/consumer-insights/baby-boomer-youtube-trends/
6   business.startsat60.com/wp-content/uploads/2019/03/Reinventing-Retirement_ThePlaybook_FM320.pdf
7   martibarletta.com/marketing-to-boomer-women-recognize-the-joy-of-being-grandma/

role as a teacher, mentor, and historian to pass on advice, traditions and customs. They value health, education and good manners. In a world that moves so quickly, they teach their grandchildren things such as holding their cutlery correctly, how to plant a tree, and cooking from scratch. The younger the grandparent, the more hands on they are.

Grandparents are providing childcare support

Grandparents are increasingly being relied on to care for their grandchildren without payment.[1] This tends to fall on grandmothers more so than grandfathers. The increased reliance on grandparents to provide childcare is the result of increasing divorce, relationship breakdowns, women returning to the workforce, and the rising costs associated with childcare.

Across Europe, 44% of grandmothers are providing childcare for their grandchildren, with grandmothers in Italy, Spain and Greece providing almost twice as much childcare as grandmothers in Sweden, France and Denmark.[2] In the UK, 40% of grandparents provide childcare support.[3] Of these, almost 90% are providing regular childcare each week. Grandmothers take on the bulk of this childcare to support their children who are working. In Australia, most grandparents are contributing approximately 30 hours each month in caring for their grandchildren.[4] A third of children of working parents are cared for by their grandparents.

Many of these grandparents are also holding down a job themselves. They are quite conflicted about their desire to spend more time with their grandchildren, but the demands of working as well are taking a toll. In the US, grandparents are heavily relied upon,

1   www.tandfonline.com/doi/full/10.1080/21582041.2018.1467034
2   grandparenteffect.com/guess-how-many-grandparents/
3   www.ageuk.org.uk/latest-news/articles/2017/september/five-million-grandparents-take-on-childcare-responsibilities/
4   www.smh.com.au/money/planning-and-budgeting/grandparents-stepping-up-as-costs-of-childcare-bite-20180531-p4zilh.html

with 25% of mothers returning to work within two weeks due to the lack of maternity leave provided by many companies.[1] AARP report that 70% of younger grandparents (44% overall) are still working as well, leading to higher levels of stress and exhaustion than in previous generations.[2]

While throughout Asia intergenerational living is common, we are seeing it become more common in western countries. In the US, 10% of American children live with a grandparent.[3] These grandparents are heavily involved in the childcare.

Purchasing behaviours

Grandparents hold significant wealth, much higher than other generations, and they typically like to make a large purchase to contribute to the arrival of their first grandchild. This is often a pram, stroller, car seat or cot, and the purchase is typically led by the grandmother. And in many cases they are buying a second pram, cot and car seat so their children don't have to cart this bulky equipment with them each time the grandchildren visit. Given their growing technical skills, don't be surprised to find grandmothers searching out the best cot in a closed Facebook group or on a review site and purchasing the product online.

Grandmothers enjoy the excitement of their new grandchild's arrival. One US study reveals that grandparents are spending US$3 billion on infant apparel alone. And their purchasing doesn't end there. They prioritise education, and often contribute to educational expenses to ensure their grandchildren receive a quality education. In Australia, different families adopt an array of educational traditions, from grandparents buying school uniforms when they start school to paying all the school fees. It means that parents aren't under such cashflow concerns and can pay it back when they

---

1   www.vox.com/2015/8/21/9188343/maternity-leave-united-states
2   marketingtomums.com.au/podcast/ep15_patty_david_grandparents_influence/
3   www.liveabout.com/facts-about-grandparents-1695849

are in a better position financially. In the US, many grandparents contribute annually to a college fund.

Generation Z's grandma impact

Contrary to widespread belief, Generation Z are listening to their family's opinions. In coming years, as they become a bigger segment of the mum market internationally, the influence of grandmothers on the purchasing decisions of Gen Z mothers will make them an even more attractive segment for marketers. It's a significant difference from the current Millennial and Generation X mothers, so there are considerable gains ahead for brands that have strong relationships with grandmothers, or who can develop them.

What are marketers getting wrong?

Grandmothers are greatly underwhelmed by brands' attempts to communicate with them. Startsat60.com reports that 85% of over 60s believed advertisers didn't understand them and their needs, with 83% of them wanting to be better understood by brands:[1] To understand this more we asked grandmothers in our #inmumswords community to tell us what they felt brands were getting wrong:

'Stop calling me a grandmother or a Baby Boomer.'

'Stop relying on outdated stereotypes. My life looks nothing like the old, grey, frumpy women you show me.'

'Where am I? I never see anyone remotely like me in advertising.'

'In Australia, advertisers and marketers typically focus their efforts on the younger generation. We like buying products and services for others, not just ourselves. We value education. We value loyalty. We value authenticity. We like to invest in

---

1   business.startsat60.com/wp-content/uploads/2019/03/Reinventing-Retirement_ThePlaybook_FM320.pdf

educational products and services, for ourselves, however not much, if any, is available to us. We don't like to be called old but we do like to know it's for people our age. We want to be informed. We don't have to save. We have money to spend. We appreciate good service but it is difficult to find.'

'Stop portraying us as technophobes who stay at home, cook and walk on the beach with our equally boring-looking husbands.'

'There seems to be a lot of sitting on couches and looking wise with very neat grey hair.'

'They assume that anyone over 50 can't wait to move into a retirement home because we are too doddery to manage a bigger property and love the idea of singalongs and bus trips.'

You can see that grandmothers are very unhappy with how they are being depicted in advertising – and that's of course if they are being depicted at all. Most grandmothers I spoke to felt they were often not even acknowledged in advertising, and if they were, they were depicted as getting ready for the nursing home. In our Marketing to Mums survey of 1800 Australian mums, we had a small but very vocal group of Baby Boomer grandmothers respond and they vocalised how misrepresented they were by brands.

Startsat60.com is an online community of people over 60 in Australia which boasts 1.68 million monthly website users. They receive almost 6.5 million pageviews each month, and have more than 770,000 in their Facebook community. Their success is that their content is perfectly pitched around travel, health and finances. They have more than 400 over-60 writers who publish an array of relevant stories. In Australia, they are the largest community of women over 55 years, and I estimate the largest online community of grandmothers in Australia.

Purchase complexity

Grandmothers have an increasing role to play in the purchase decisions of the family that is not being fully realised in the market right now. The reliance on grandmothers to provide childcare coupled with the rise in intergenerational living arrangements has led to them making purchases previously thought to be untaken only by parents. Grandmothers might be doing the weekly shopping for nappies, school snack foods and baby formula as the parents are working. This is resulting in greater complexity in the path to purchase for many brands.

Furthermore, new opportunities are presenting due to grandparents' increasing role in the family. Grandmothers are often behind buying a new car that will accommodate their grandchildren. They are buying new SUVs and station wagons typically marketed to families. There is a strong focus on safety. This seems a missed opportunity in the automotive industry.

Nits are a thing for grandmothers. With their increased role in childcare, grandparents are at risk of childhood inconveniences such as nits. If you are going to really get rid of nits then grandparents also need to be treated.

I have witnessed this trend in my own family life. My mother, a grandmother of six, is almost 78 years old. She retired from work in her early 70s after a successful career as a training consultant. She looks after two of her grandchildren up to three days each week as both parents work, and she chooses to spend her free time in yoga classes and down at the beach. For six weeks of the year she travels to New York to listen to jazz and spend time with her sister. She's recently upgraded her car, with safety the top priority as she frequently drives her grandchildren, and she wanted to ensure her new car had Bluetooth so she could speak on her mobile phone hands free. She is referred to as 'Nin Nin' as opposed to grandma, as she felt that made her sound old. She likes it as it's as unique as she is.

Chapter 4: The big opportunities in the mum market

- Women over 45 who are working and balancing the needs of dependent older children and the increasing health needs of their aging parents feel overlooked by the media and brands.

- There have never been more single mothers in the world than right now. Single mums have emerged as a powerful segment who are overlooked by most brands.

- Today's mothers are looking for tech-first solutions to their problems. Mothers are spending more and more time on the internet, primarily via smartphones.

- If you want to stay relevant you'll need to understand Generation Z.

- Mums in business are an untapped, growing segment among the professional services market which many brands are overlooking.

- Migrant mums – those not born in the country in which they reside – represent a largely untapped opportunity. They are a compelling and overlooked market.

- Pregnant women and first-time mothers are a highly desired audience. Brands can start their relationships with expectant mothers and join them throughout parenthood.

- Grandmothers have an increasing role to play in the purchase decisions of the family that is not being fully realised in the market.

KEY POINTS

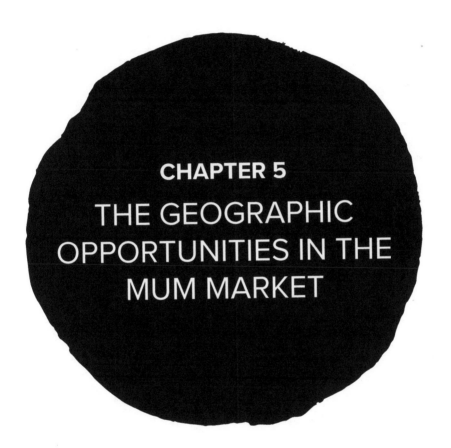

CHAPTER 5

THE GEOGRAPHIC OPPORTUNITIES IN THE MUM MARKET

Many companies are looking abroad for their future growth. While there exists growth potential in many locations around the world, I've decided to focus on five of the biggest opportunities I see in the marketplace right now: China, India, Indonesia, the US and the UK. In this chapter I provide you with some key considerations and potentially very profitable opportunities in the mum markets in these countries, and I hope to spark interest in further research to evaluate if any of these locations are suitable for your brand.

China

There were more than 15 million babies born in China in 2018, down from the 17 million peak in 2017, yet still representing an enormous opportunity for brands. To put this into perspective, this is almost four times the number of babies born in the US. Coupled with the great volume of babies being born in China is a growing middle class, making Millennial mothers a very lucrative market for many brands.

According to a 2018 Nielsen report, Chinese mothers make 90% of the purchase decisions related to the child, making the mum market very attractive.[1] Azoya Consulting note a study by Frost & Sullivan and Babytree which highlights that the mother is the primary decision maker when it comes to any financial decisions within the family.[2] AdAge China reports that there are 320 million working mothers in China.[3] These women are enjoying advancing careers, are highly educated, and want the best available for themselves and their family. If you want your brand to capitalise on this massive opportunity, you are going to need to influence the purchase behaviour of Chinese mothers.

---

1   www.nielsen.com/cn/en/insights/news/2019/challenges-and-new-opportunities-in-mother-and-infant-market.html
2   www.azoyagroup.com/blog/view/how-to-capitalize-on-chinas-booming-mom-baby-sector/
3   adage.com/china/article/special-report/what-chinese-mothers-want-from-your-brand/143061

Family structure and dynamics

With the abolition of the one-child policy in 2015 in favour of a two-child policy, China is encouraging families to grow. While the total number of babies has recently declined, there is still strong interest in taking advantage of the new policy. One Chinese study has identified that more than 73% of Millennial parents were interested in having a second child.[1] The level of interest is dependent on family wealth. The subject of whether to have a second child attracts significant online discussion in mothers' groups, including on Weibo. There exists a very different family dynamic in China. The majority of Chinese mothers engage in a 30- to 45-day confinement period after the birth of a child. They are often residing in confinement centres where they are to focus on their recovery, and they are allowed to do very little. Alternatively, a nurse comes to live with the family for a month. The confinement period represents an ancient tradition known as 'zuo yue zi' or 'sitting the month', where new mothers remain indoors and healing foods are prepared for them. They are to focus on bonding with their child and healing their body after childbirth. Visitors are often not permitted for at least the first 12 days after the baby is born.

The majority of Chinese mothers return to work soon after having a child. A GlobalWebIndex 2018 report found that 80% of Chinese mothers work fulltime, with only 10% being a stay-at-home mother.[2] As such, grandparents are heavily involved in the day-to-day family activities. Essentially, with a Chinese family you should be considering the mother, father, child, and two sets of grandparents.

---

1   www.azoyagroup.com/blog/view/how-to-capitalize-on-chinas-booming-mom-baby-sector/
2   www.globalwebindex.com/hubfs/Downloads/Marketing-to-Moms-eBook.pdf

Smartphone use

eMarketer reports that Chinese Millennial mothers have the highest smartphone penetration across the world.[1] They are early adopters of technology, so it's imperative that you take a tech-first mother approach to your marketing strategy. They use their smartphones extensively to research, interact and purchase products. The research phase of the purchase decision making is far deeper in China as they seek out your product authenticity and quality, and this happens from their phone.

Social media

WeChat is the social media platform most used by mothers in China; 66% of Chinese mums use it, which is higher than the rest of the Chinese population.[2] It supports the understanding that women increase their use of social media once they become mothers. Chinese mothers like to share WeChat moments, connect with friends and to make shopping payments, with WeChat now processing one billion payments every day.[3] WeChat has become instrumental in the success of many luxury brands that are targeting affluent working mothers. Weibo is another social media platform popular among Chinese mothers. It's closest western comparison would be Twitter. QQ is extremely popular among younger Chinese, so this is another social media platform to be aware of for the Chinese mothers of tomorrow. It is very entertainment focused and particularly well used by students – it is a social media platform to watch.

A 2018 Kantar study found that electronic coupons were a big attraction for Chinese mums conducting online shopping.[4] The report found Chinese mothers are 54% more likely to search for and download electronic coupons onto their mobile phone. Brands

---

1 www.emarketer.com/Article/How-Mobile-Millennial-Mothers-China/1012241
2 www.globalwebindex.com/hubfs/Downloads/Marketing-to-Moms-eBook.pdf
3 www.springwise.com/top-takeaways-from-the-2019-world-retail-congress?utm_campaign=1494016_Springwise%20Edit%202019-May-29&utm_medium=email&utm_source=Newsletter&dm_i=3GJ2,W0SG,5RTNKE,3C0XV,1
4 uk.kantar.com/media/668931/globaltgidispatches18_uk.pdf

operating in this market or considering entry should be considering how they can use coupons to influence sales.

Shopping behaviours

Shopping centres, specialty stores and department stores remain the biggest channel for brands selling to mothers, however e-commerce is seeing rapid growth. Given Chinese mothers are likely to be working, they are increasingly turning to online marketplaces to source goods, including Tmall, JD, Taobao and Dandang. This is leading to huge growth in ecommerce platforms. Online now represents 16% of overall sales in the maternity and baby sector, and is growing at 30% per annum.[1] This growth is expected to continue until at least 2022. Mothers from tier 1 cities feel the most comfortable with online shopping.

Quality and heritage matters

Quality is the key driver in purchasing for both pregnant women and mothers, particularly in the baby category. Safety is also important if selling in the infant category, after the infant formula poisoning scandals in 2008. Quality outweighs pricing concerns, with shipping times only being of small consideration. A 2019 GlobalWebIndex survey of 2000 US and Chinese mothers found that two out of three new mothers in China would pay more for baby food if they considered it to be of higher quality. This was significantly higher than US mothers.[2] For overseas brands entering the market, Chinese mothers want to know the historical background of your brand. Heritage really matters in China. It's vital that brands consider marketing to Chinese parents within their own country *before* or, at the very least, at the same time as they start their move into China. Chinese parents will check the authenticity,

---

1 www.azoyagroup.com/blog/view/how-to-capitalize-on-chinas-booming-mom-baby-sector/
2 www.digitalmarketingcommunity.com/researches/marketing-to-u-s-and-chinese-moms-in-2019-globalwebindex/

reputation, heritage and quality of a brand through their contacts in the country of origin before considering a purchase.[1] I have recently worked with an Australian based company who have built their product for the Chinese market. The purpose of my engagement was to assist them develop their profile amongst Australian mothers, specifically Australian Chinese migrant mothers, as they recognise that prospective Chinese customers will research and seek out evidence of the company's success in their home country prior to purchase in China.

The role of daigous

Given that Chinese mothers are looking for endorsement of your brand in your country of origin, consideration should be given to marketing to the Chinese community within your own country as part of your marketing strategy into China. Daigous represent an underdeveloped opportunity for brands to do this. Daigous are people who purchase international products on behalf of their customers in China. They are typically Chinese university students who are purchasing products for Chinese customers and shipping them home. Chinese shoppers rely on daigous to provide reputable, high-quality products, thus acting as a strong endorsement for your brand. A recent Nielsen report estimated that there are between 40,000 and 100,000 daigous operating in Australia, responsible for up to $100 billion annually in product sales.[2] There is trust in daigous that brands can tap into. It represents a significant and developed sales channel for brands that is not yet maximised.

1   www.abc.net.au/news/rural/2019-05-30/how-three-australian-businesses-cracked-the-chinese-market/11158948
2   www.nielsen.com/au/en/insights/report/2017/the-daigou-effect-how-brands-can-break-down-chinese-borders-and-drive-growth/

Third-party proof

Chinese mothers rely heavily on testimonials. They actively head online to seek out recommendations from industry experts and other mums to sway their purchase decisions. It can help them reduce their purchase consideration set and remove fraudulent products. Online forums for mothers are a key source to find third-party proof, with Babytree, MamaWang and MamaBang popular.

The role of influencers

Influencers – also known as key opinion leaders (KOLs) – play a large role in the purchasing decisions of Chinese mothers. Influencers are treated with enormous respect in China by companies; brands tend to seek out long-term partnerships with the influencers they work with. Brands seek to leverage the respect and sway an influencer has in their community. Mothers generally have a few select influencers they follow who assist them to narrow their search for products and services. Fees are high, so this approach tends to be reserved for larger brands. This is a tried-and-tested strategy to effectively build trust among Chinese mothers.

Market entry considerations for China

Catherine Cervasio launched Aromababy Natural Skincare in Australia in 1994, where she pioneered the natural and organic personal care space. In 2007 she launched into the Chinese market. Catherine believes success in China does not happen quickly:

> 'While potentially lucrative, China is a highly competitive market attracting interest from brand owners around the world. There are various "tier" cities based on population and economic outlook. The tier 1 cities, for example Shanghai and Beijing, are incredibly difficult to break into due to fierce global appeal. These tier 1 cities are often favoured by larger companies who have the capacity to invest heavily in order to

build brand awareness, or for global brands who have already
built a strong identity. There is, however, enormous opportunity
in lower tier cities. In China there are 160 cities, each with over
one million people. In my experience often lesser known brands
will gain more traction by targeting a lower tier city, even 3 or 4,
where consumer demand for imported product is high yet access
to "choice" is far less, compared to, say, in Beijing.'

One way to stand out, according to Catherine, is to have a strong
point of difference and brand story, as she explains:

'In China you need to find a way to stand out from the
thousands of other products on shelves or online. This
is particularly critical if you are a premium brand like
Aromababy. We will never be able to compete on price when
compared to an imported mass-market or Chinese-made baby
lotion, so there needs to be something more. Chinese business
owners and consumers alike love a strong brand story that is
both authentic and unique. They will search your brand online
and will feel confident when they see it has 10 or more years
behind it. They want to be sure you're on shelves in your own
country, and elsewhere. For us, having Aromababy in Hong
Kong and Singapore for 20 years has strong appeal and helps to
build trust. Add to this that buyers can see photos and business
articles to show that I have invested time and effort over more
than a decade in the market, running workshops for mothers
and midwives, adding value in my small way to the Chinese
community, it's no surprise Aromababy has been embraced.'

Western brands also need to understand they are invisible to mothers in mainland China due to the government's digital firewall, so
the first thing brands need to do is recreate their digital assets for
visibility in China. This starts by gaining the relevant trademarks,
having a Chinese website, and then gaining visibility through the

main Chinese search engines: Baidu, Sogou, 360 and Shenma. Facebook is not visible in China, and mothers favour WeChat. It's recommended that you partner with a China marketing firm to guide you in creating your digital footprint in China and assisting you to create a strategic marketing plan.

Forming strategic partnerships

The mother and baby category has seen considerable success for overseas brands that use strategic partnerships.

Gerber – a US brand owned by Nestlé, and one of America's oldest baby food brands – has enjoyed considerable success in China. Gerber is highly desired for their safe and high-quality baby food offering. Gerber's commitment to high quality has resulted in them being the number one baby food brand in China. Gerber built a strategic partnership with Tmall, Alibaba's marketplace. Having being founded in 1920s in the US, Gerber enjoys a strong heritage which is highly valued by Chinese mothers. They trust the brand, and this has allowed Gerber to establish a premium-priced baby food positioning.

Bubs Australia was founded by mum of three Kristy Carr in 2006 from her kitchen at home while on maternity leave. Twelve years later they represent Australia's largest producer of goat dairy products. Bubs Australia focus on the first 1000 days of life, with a range of infant formula, organic baby food and organic toddler snacks. They have a focus on the Chinese market. They have enjoyed exceptional revenue increases in recent years as they form strategic partnerships with leading distributors and promoters within China. They also tap into the daigou market in Australia to promote their products back to mainland China. Bubs's upward trajectory really commenced after securing Chinese investment and board representation.

India

By 2024, India is expected to overtake China and become the world's most populated country.[1] According to the World Economic Forum, India will have 1.5 billion people by 2100, more than three times the population of the US.[2]

Every year almost 27 million babies are born in India.[3] This is more than the entire population of Australia, with 90% of these babies born to Millennial women. They represent 20% of the world's births. Coupled with this, there is a growing middle class, which is expected to be the largest segment of the population by 2022.[4] They are increasingly spending more on their children – up 13% each year.

India increasingly represents a highly attractive market for companies looking for significant growth, with many distinguishing characteristics and behaviours. But with 23 official languages and a dispersed middle class, there are also many issues to consider and challenges that need to be overcome when entering the Indian market. Let's take a look at some of these.

Massive internet use by mums

One of the most striking characteristics of Indian mothers is their reliance on the internet. The 2018 'Asian Digital Mum Survey' by Tickled Media, owner of theAsianparent, found that for 87% of Indian mothers the internet is an important part of their lives. But what is particularly significant is how their media consumption changes once becoming a parent, with a whopping 71% reporting an increase in internet searches and a decrease in traditional media

1 www.insideretail.com.au/news/indias-e-commerce-baby-boom-201808
2 www.weforum.org/agenda/2018/02/these-will-be-the-worlds-most-populated-countries-by-2100
3 www.medindia.net/patients/calculators/pop_clock.asp
4 www.pwc.in/research-insights/2018/propelling-india-towards-global-leadership-in-e-commerce.html

use.[1] Like their counterparts across the world, Indian mothers are using the internet to seek our parenting information, predominantly from other mums, with Indian mothers seven times more likely to interact with other mothers online than in real life. They are seeking a mobile-first solution to their problems. This is a significant insight if you are considering an entry into the Indian market.

Social media

Social media is particularly popular among Indian mothers.[2] The top three social media accounts an Indian mum is likely to have are Facebook, Instagram and YouTube. Facebook has particularly high penetration, with some reports claiming that India is the biggest Facebook market in the world.[3] Tickled Media report that 94% of Indian mothers have a Facebook account. It's a big gap between Facebook and the other platforms; 56% of Indian mothers have an Instagram account and 41% have a YouTube account.

WhatsApp deserves a mention also.[4] It represents a popular platform which has gathered more than 200 million users across India. It has proved particularly popular among older mums and grandmothers, who enjoy sending a 'good morning' message to their adult children each day.[5] They find it less complicated than Facebook. It is also well used by mothers to manage school and class communications. I read about one mother who had to put her WhatsApp account on silent as she received in excess of 40 messages per hour.[6]

---

1 www.digitalmarket.asia/engagement-key-to-reaching-indias-growing-number-of-mothers-online/

2 www.digitalmarket.asia/engagement-key-to-reaching-indias-growing-number-of-mothers-online/

3 www.socialmediatoday.com/social-business/facebooks-expansion-indonesia-and-opportunities-provides-infographic

4 www.buzzfeednews.com/article/pranavdixit/older-indians-drive-millennials-crazy-on-whatsapp-this-is

5 www.bbc.com/news/world-asia-india-42801115

6 scroll.in/magazine/834036/indian-schools-are-using-whatsapp-to-enslave-mothers-and-crush-childrens-independence

Online communities

Indian mothers seek out connection with other mothers in online communities built just for mums. These communities represent their trusted network, and they are heavily influenced by the recommendations they receive.

Baby Destination is one of the more popular online communities for mothers in India. The company was founded by Tamanna Dhamija in 2015 after the birth of her first child, when she found it difficult to source the information she needed that was free from judgement. She walked away from her corporate finance career in New York to move back to India and start up an online community where mums could obtain parenting advice from other caring women.[1] Initially they focused on tier 1 cities, but they are now focusing on catering for tier 2 and 3 cities, and partner with many brands wanting to connect with Indian mothers. Baby Destination predominantly caters for Millennial mothers, and now reaches 15 million mums throughout India every month. Tamanna has plans to grow the business to reach 100 million Indian mothers within a decade.

Online shopping

While coming off a relatively low base, ecommerce is enjoying exponential growth in India due to increasing internet penetration. Bain & Company report a 53% increase between 2013 and 2017. Popular online marketplaces include FirstCry.com, Reliance, Flipkart (recently acquired by Walmart), Amazon and Alibaba.

To date, the ecommerce industry has catered strongly for a male audience and has been very discount driven. There is enormous opportunity in catering for Indian Millennial mothers seeking convenience and discount offers in the coming years. It represents

---

1 www.businessworld.in/article/An-Idea-Born-Out-Of-A-Need-Tamanna-Dhamija-Baby-Destination/08-03-2019-167961/

an increasingly attractive option for brands that see it as an efficient way to reach a dispersed middle-class segment of mothers. Online penetration is currently lower than other Asian markets, but this is dynamically evolving and new growth is expected to be fuelled by expansion into tier 2 and 3 cities and targeting of both Millennial and Generation X mothers. Fashion and beauty are fast-growing categories.[1] Morgan Stanley estimates that India's ecommerce industry will be valued at US$200 billion by 2027.

Child-first approach

According to a 2016 'Frank About Women' report, one of the defining behaviours of Indian mothers is the extent to which they place their child first over themselves.[2] This is significantly different from Australian and American mothers, who feel more comfortable with a mother-first approach. Given this insight, it's not surprising that Indian mothers are 95% more likely to encourage their children to reach milestones ahead of schedule as compared to mums in other countries.

This provides significant insight into the appetite for educational products and services catering for children. It also highlights the need for brands to celebrate Indian mothers' selflessness in their communications. This was achieved by Swiggy, an Indian food delivery service that wanted to honour mums in their 2019 Mother's Day video campaign. The video showcases the difference between what mum says and what she really means. It taps into an Indian mother's deep and selfless love for her children. The campaign went viral immediately.

---

1 timesofindia.indiatimes.com/business/india-business/india-is-fastest-growing-e-commerce-market-report/articleshow/66857926.cms
2 www.frankaboutwomen.com/wp-content/uploads/2016/06/frank-about-women-global-motherhood-study-us-ver.pdf

Gender inequality is a major issue in India

Gender inequality is a significant issue in India. A patriarchal society, mothers across the country carry out the bulk of unpaid work caring for children and carrying out domestic duties. This has impacted their ability to participate in paid work. It's not surprising then to hear Forbes report that women comprise only 27% of the workforce (by comparison, the participation rate globally is 40%). Efforts to address this have included the recent legislative amendment to increase maternity leave from 12 to 26 weeks.[1] Employers are starting to focus on supporting mothers returning to work also, and many online communities for women regularly highlight the great achievements of working mothers. Four Indian working mothers were recently featured on the Forbes 100 Most Powerful Women list:

- Arundhati Bhattacharya, Managing Director of the State Bank of India

- Chanda Kochhar, CEO of ICICI Bank

- Indra Nooyi, CEO of PepsiCo

- Shobhna Bhartia, Chair of HT Media.[2]

Mums carry the domestic load

Indian mothers are reported to do 15 times more housework than the men in the house. Modern Indian mothers do this with great reluctance. They love it when brands take their point of view and champion gender equality for them. In 2015, P&G Company launched 'Share the Load' campaigns for their Ariel laundry detergent. It called on men to stand up and get more involved in domestic duties. These campaigns have been incredibly successful, and are now in their third season. They have gone a long way in

---

1 www.forbes.com/sites/sindhujabalaji/2018/05/18/these-indian-startups-are-making-it-easier-for-mothers-to-return-to-work-after-maternity-leave/#6ec49fbb3b5f
2 www.theindusparent.com/four-indian-working-mums-among-the-100-most-powerful-women-in-the-world

building rapport and loyalty for the company among Indian mothers.[1]

Market entry considerations for India

Storytelling is incredibly effective for connecting with Indian mothers. It connects to the heart and quickly builds rapport. Sharing stories is integral to Indian life, and this needs to be understood and reflected in brand communications. Successful campaigns, such as 'Share the Load' and Swiggy, share stories that honour Indian mothers and focus on their selfless nature.

Indonesia

Indonesia is the largest nation in Southeast Asia and the fourth most populated country in the world.[2] With a burgeoning middle class and a GDP sitting at 5% growth, it represents a growing opportunity for many brands.[3] It has a youthful population, with approximately half of Indonesians aged under 30. Australian brands are well positioned to service the boundless potential that exists in servicing Indonesian mothers, however they must have a local partner or engage a local distributor to sell into this market.

Buying power and influence

There are great opportunities for brands to establish a presence in this emerging market, which isn't getting the media attention of China and India, and there are many similarities between Australian and Indonesian mothers in their online behaviours and preferences. In 2018 Tickled Media – owner of theAsianparent – undertook a survey of more than 1000 mothers living in Indonesia to better understand their digital behaviours and emerging trends.[4]

---

1   www.socialsamosa.com/2019/02/making-of-ariel-share-the-load/
2   www.austrade.gov.au/australian/export/export-markets/countries/indonesia/industries/consumer-goods
3   asialinkbusiness.com.au/country/indonesia
4   issuu.com/theasianparent/docs/tap_survey_report-110917

Indonesian mothers identified themselves as the 'Chief Household Officer', influencing 98% of household purchasing. Other findings included:

- Indonesian mothers are mobile first, favouring Android, with low use of laptops or tablets.

- Indonesian mothers reduce their traditional media consumption significantly after the birth of their first child.

- Television viewing drops sharply after the birth of the child, and remains at low levels until the child reaches the age of four.

Indonesia mothers rely on parenting websites and social media for their product information and recommendations. They are seeking parenting tips, cooking, news and health tips.

Social media is huge

Social media is the fastest and most effective way to reach Indonesian mothers, with a staggering 99% of Indonesian mothers having a social media account, with Facebook being the most popular in 2017. A whopping 19% of Indonesian mums claim to be on Facebook more than 10 hours each day.[1] Indonesians are much more active on Facebook, reportedly commenting 60% more than the global average and sharing content at three times the global average.[2] They follow brands to keep up with new products and find discounts on products. Like Australian mothers, they enjoy spending the bulk of their time on Facebook in the evening. Indonesian mothers also like to speak with other mums via closed Facebook groups.

However, in 2018 we saw a strong shift in social media use with Instagram overtaking Facebook to become the favourite social

---

1 issuu.com/theasianparent/docs/tap_survey_report-110917
2 www.socialmediatoday.com/social-business/facebooks-expansion-indonesia-and-opportunities-provides-infographic

media platform among Indonesian mums. The Indonesian Digital Mum survey reveals 33% of Indonesian mums are spending more than five hours each day engaging on the platform. It has also become one of their favourite places to engage in online shopping also.[1] There is low use of Snapchat.

Messaging apps are also very popular among Indonesian mums. They identify WhatsApp as their favourite messaging app, followed by LINE, Facebook Messenger and Telegram.[2]

Apps spending

Southeast Asia leads the way in spending in apps, with a Criteo report revealing that 54% of all online spending is happening in-app.[3] Indonesia has embraced 'super apps' in a big way. Go-Jek and Grab are the two ride hailing Asian start-ups that have valuations over $10 billion.[4] Go-Jek is a highly successful Indonesian start-up, while Grab is a Singaporean-based business operating throughout Asia – it processes more than six million ride orders every day. They aggressively launched into Indonesia in 2018. Grab seeks to secure market leadership in the lucrative Indonesian market. In 2017, Go-Jek launched Go-Life, a super app that allows users to order food and lifestyle services all from the one app. Given the high level of convenience and efficiency they deliver, they have been quickly adopted by Indonesian mothers who value convenience. While researching this book I spoke with a friend who was on an assignment in Indonesia, who reported that these super apps allow you to 'order a cab or motorcycle taxi, food, supermarket shopping, a nail and hair beautician to come to your house,

1   http://green-indonesia.org/pluginfile.php/24650/mod_resource/content/1/star-Indonesian_Digital_Mum_Survey_2018-Presentation_deck.pdf

2   http://green-indonesia.org/pluginfile.php/24650/mod_resource/content/1/star-Indonesian_Digital_Mum_Survey_2018-Presentation_deck.pdf

3   insideretail.asia/2018/06/19/southeast-asian-online-shoppers-lead-the-world-in-spending-via-apps/

4   fortune.com/longform/grab-gojek-super-apps/

a house cleaner and a car wash. It's totally amazing. This app is the starting point for understanding Indonesian mothers.'

Go-Jek is reported to have 25 million monthly users and to process more than 100 million transactions, providing employment for more than a million drivers.[1]

Grab offers numerous services spanning healthcare, food delivery, financial services and digital payments. They are actively offering discount promotions to lure users towards their app, which appears to be working, with downloads outperforming Go-Jek in the first three months of 2019.[2]

Online shopping

Ecommerce is rapidly developing in Indonesia.[3] Mothers, who are particularly tech savvy, are the early adopters of ecommerce in Indonesia. The 'Digital Mom and Baby Shopper Profile' in Indonesia – a survey of more than 1100 mothers – in 2018 found 66% of mums had made a baby purchase online.[4] New and younger mothers value the convenience offered by shopping online, the most popular ecommerce websites being Shopee, Lazada (both market-places) and Tokopedia, where baby clothing and baby gear are the most popular categories. It is not widely used for food or things for mums, where traditional channels such as department stores and shopping malls are still popular. Harbolnas is the national shopping day, held on 12 December. It was launched in 2012; it has quickly grown to become a great opportunity for brands.[5]

Religious events impact online sales in Indonesia. According to a Criteo study, Ramadan is increasing online spending in Indonesia,

1 fortune.com/longform/grab-gojek-super-apps/
2 asia.nikkei.com/Spotlight/Sharing-Economy/Grab-vs-Go-Jek-Duel-of-digital-decacorns-escalates-in-Indonesia
3 www.austrade.gov.au/australian/export/export-markets/countries/indonesia/industries/consumer-goods
4 techsauce.co/en/tech-and-biz/66-of-indonesias-female-population-and-mothers-to-be-are-shopping-online-and-open-to-trying-new-baby-brands/
5 us.kantar.com/business/brands/2018/top-50-most-valuable-indonesian-brands-2018/

with sales increasing in the lead up to and during Ramadan but declining towards Eid al-Fitr, which marks the end of Ramadan. Interestingly, sales slow during fasting, however lift once the fast is broken, so timing of offers is a consideration.[1,2]

When selling in Indonesia, it's important to realise that less than 4% of the population resides in Jakarta. The country comprises more than 17,500 islands. Just like China, there are many regional areas which have very different tastes.[3] Success in Indonesia requires marketing strategies that are tailored to the relevant regional area, which can present some challenges.

The role of testimonials

Testimonials strongly influence mums' online purchase behaviour. With the high level of time spent on Facebook, it's critical that brands look to implement a strong strategy to encourage testimonials and ensure these are highlighted on both Facebook and Instagram, the two favoured social media platforms for mums. TheAsianparent's 2018 'Indonesian Digital Mums' report found that 98% of Indonesian mums had bought something because of an internet recommendation.[4] A strong testimonial strategy is key to entry into the Indonesian market and appealing to mothers.

Beauty and wellness

Austrade identifies Indonesia as the fastest growing beauty and wellness market in Asia. Much like China, they seek high-quality natural and organic beauty products. The beauty sector has experienced double-digit growth in Indonesia, with mothers being

1   insideretail.asia/2019/04/24/ramadan-an-opportunity-for-retailers-online-research-reveals/#daily

2   insideretail.asia/2017/04/13/ramadan-online-shopping-trends-revealed/

3   us.kantar.com/business/brands/2018/top-50-most-valuable-indonesian-brands-2018/

4   http://green-indonesia.org/pluginfile.php/24650/mod_resource/content/1/star-Indonesian_Digital_Mum_Survey_2018-Presentation_deck.pdf

very brand conscious. There is huge demand for halal-certified and herbal beauty products.[1]

Brand success

Monique Filer and Dannielle Michaels started b.box in 2007 after a frustrating experience changing a baby on a plane between Australia and New Zealand. It led to the creation of their first product, a baby box containing the essentials for changing your baby. B.box has now grown into a range of juvenile products known for innovation, quality and creativity in product design, including sippy cups and feeding products. B.box are positioned as fun, functional and affordable. The company has enjoyed incredible growth and strong traction in high-growth markets, including China and Korea. Today their products are sold in 35 countries across Asia-Pacific, Europe, the US and the Middle East, and in South Africa. Last year they moved into the Indonesian market, partnering with a local distributor and I spoke with Dannielle Michaels about their experience so far:

'Indonesia is a new market for b.box but we have already seen the excitement the brand has generated. Indonesia has a fast-growing middle class with the financial capacity and desire for access to more international brands. They want international brands that deliver good design and trendy quality products for their babies. They love that b.box is Australian and has a reputation for high-quality design and performance. Our distributor is investing in brand building through social media and online, and is featuring b.box in consumer shows and showcases our brand nationally. We know it can take a couple of years to gain market penetration, but we are confident that

---

1   martinroll.com/resources/articles/strategy/the-asian-beauty-industry-new-challenges-and-opportunities/

b.box will be the name mums mention when discussing leading feeding and drinking options for their bubs and children.'

The United States

There are 85 million mothers in the US who are responsible for US$2.4 trillion in spending annually.[1] Every year four million babies are born; 40% of these are to first-time mothers. The US mum market is large, educated, technically savvy and still has plenty of scope for growth. Yet, like many mothers across the globe, US mums are feeling dissatisfied with brands because of the inaccurate way they represent them in advertising. One study revealed that 56% of American mums believe marketers don't understand them.[2] This represents an enormous growth opportunity for smart businesses. The US market is popular with Australian brands looking for more profits and growth. The market size is attractive, and they see fewer cultural obstacles compared to Asia. As an Australian-based marketing consultancy, I provide advisory services for companies and boards wanting to expand into the US market. I typically help them with key introductions and educate them about core differences between mothers in the US versus Australia. Essentially, I prepare them for growth and then hand them over to some of the trusted marketing connections I have developed since starting Marketing to Mums. One of the brands I'm working with is Australia's largest preschool ballet school, Tiny Tutus. Launched in 2009, with more than 100 studios across Australia their CEO Simone Lindus now feels the time is right to expand overseas, and she sees America as a key opportunity:

'We've been watching the US dance studio industry for the last couple of years and have seen the steady growth. With

---

1   www.m2moms.com/fast-facts/
2   www.mdgadvertising.com/marketing-insights/infographics/how-to-market-to-moms-5-insights-for-brands-infographic/

the dance industry expected to reach US$4 billion in revenue in 2019 and more than half of that coming from ballet classes, there has never been a better time to share Tiny Tutus with the US. When email enquiries about our curriculum and programs started coming in from the US over the last 12 months, we knew that taking Tiny Tutus to the US was the perfect next step.'

Educated, working and financially independent mums

American mothers are well educated. The *New York Times* cites a Pew report which found 80% of professional women with degrees have a child by age 44, up from 65% 20 years ago.[1] They are active participants in the workforce, with 71% working, up from 47% in 1975.[2] Increasingly they are financially independent, with women being the primary or only breadwinner in 40% of households with children under 18.[3] Being under pressure, American mothers are more likely to turn to parenting experts and online forums for advice than European mothers.

Stress and worry are high in US mums

American mothers are suffering significant stress and worry a lot. There is a lack of support for working mothers in America. With the absence of paid maternity leave, 25% of mums are back at work within two weeks of their child's birth. For those not ready, they are relying on their saved annual leave to assist in healing after birth before returning to work, only not being able to take a break later in the year is then adding to their exhaustion. On top of this, they face the 'mother load', those extra four hours a day of keeping on top of running the household. These stresses in their day-to-day living

---

1   www.nytimes.com/2018/01/18/upshot/the-us-fertility-rate-is-down-yet-more-women-are-mothers.html
2   www.pewresearch.org/fact-tank/2014/05/09/5-questions-and-answers-about-american-moms-today/
3   www.mdgadvertising.com/marketing-insights/infographics/how-to-market-to-moms-5-insights-for-brands-infographic/

are changing the way American mothers shop. They are prioritising convenience and efficiency, even if this comes at a small premium.

Worry is another emotion mums feel – a lot. In 2017–18, 4.2 million US school students as young as kindergarten age experienced a lockdown drill. They worry about what has happened in a society that has seen school shootings become common, and what kind of world their child is growing up in. And mums worry about their children being traumatised by the drill itself. It weighs heavily on them. This particular worry is especially acute in the US as the country grapples with the issue of gun violence.[1]

Online communities

Online communities dedicated to American mums or parents have proved very effective in building awareness and deepening relationships between mums and brands. Two US-based online communities excelling in this area with excellent engagement are Raising Dragons and What's up Moms?

In 2018 I met Andrea Scalzo Yi – an engineering major and former retail fashion executive for Donna Karan – at a conference where we were both speaking. As the mum of four boys aged under 10, she is the founder of Raising Dragons, a cross-platform destination that features short videos of simple science, technology, engineering, art and maths (STEAM) activities. Launched in 2017, it has amassed more than 800,000 fans and more than 50 million video views, all organically. Andrea's success has been in her ability to offer parents and educators simple activities that do not require a trip to the craft shop, utilising materials that are likely to be available in your house. Andrea's content is clearly valued by parents wanting to create fun, playful learning environments for their children.

---

1 www.theatlantic.com/magazine/archive/2019/03/active-shooter-drills-erika-christakis/580426/

What's Up Moms, a YouTube parenting channel, was dreamt up four years ago by Stanford University friends Elle Walker and Meg Resnikoff, after they had difficulty finding video content to assist them in being parents. Since launching, they have attracted more than 2.6 million subscribers to their YouTube channel, which generates more than 60 million video views every month (and over a billion views to date). Forbes have ranked them number one 'parenting influencer' in the US. Their success can be attributed to a deep understanding of their audience. They use fun, playful communications which are not only entertaining but provide real value. Using mums' desire to save time has seen them produce a series of 'mum hacks' which generate enormous interest, with one video having 18 million views alone on where to park your car when you go shopping, through to art and craft activity hacks with 48 million views. With figures like these, it's no surprise they have become a go-to advertising partner for many brands, including Target, Disney, Tide and Clinique.

African Americans: an emerging powerhouse

Representing 14% of the American population, African Americans are an emerging powerhouse in the US economy. A Nielsen study reports that their purchasing power is expected to rise to US$1.54 trillion by 2022, outpacing the growth of non-Hispanic whites.[1] Mothers are the gate keepers into African American households. To find out more, I spoke to Christine Michel Carter, a global marketing strategist and Forbes contributor who specialises in helping brands better understand the buying power of black consumers:

'American mothers control 85% of household purchases and have a spending power of $2.4 trillion, but people of color hold a growing share of buying power in the US at $1.5 trillion, with

---

1 www.nielsen.com/us/en/insights/reports/2018/from-consumers-to-creators.html

black spending power growing seven percentage points higher than white spending power. Black moms are an attractive consumer because they not only control what black millennial men spend their money on, but due to their ability to influence other generations (sometimes within their household) they also control what other generations (Baby Boomers, Generation X) spend their money on too.

'I've researched six growth opportunities for brands, basically ways they can leverage maternal black girl magic. Brands can tap into the black mother's ability to influence across generations, our free-thinking spirit (as content creators, consultants and diverse team members), our love of self-care (emotional and physical) and the fact that we're social mamas who spend more time on social networking sites engaging with brands and social causes than other races. Though black moms are brand-loyal consumers ... brands must positively reflect our community in branding, packaging and advertising. This brings me to the two other growth opportunities, which are admittedly harder to execute. They include understanding that we're political parents: it's important for a brand not to ignore the realities of today's America. We also put family first. Our family includes our online and offline community, family and friends. Brands must make sure they're giving back to and do no harm to our environment, community, family, and health.'

African Americans are technology lovers. They are more likely than the rest of the US population to own a smart speaker, smart watch, wireless headphones, smart TV, smartphone, tablet, or use an internet-to-TV streaming service. And it doesn't stop there. They are more likely than the rest of the population to listen to a podcast, use video-streaming services and voice assistants, and engage with digital wallets. They are incredibly quick to adopt new technologies. New African American mothers fall into our tech-first mums category (see chapter 4), seeking out tech solutions to support them in parenthood.[1] The high use of tech and the internet sees them embrace online shopping. Additionally, African Americans believe brands should support social causes at higher rates than non-Hispanic whites. They represent a growing opportunity for many brands.

The United Kingdom

Mothers living in the UK are powerful and influential consumers, responsible for £205 billion in spending every year.[2] Yet these mothers are dismayed and fed up with brands, with only 19% being able to relate to the way they are depicted in advertising.[3] Better understanding mothers in the UK and accurately representing them in your marketing communications could give your brand the edge over others, and is ever so simple.

UK mums are digitally reliant

Like mothers across the world, UK mothers are digitally active. Saatchi & Saatchi report 96% of UK mothers use the internet compared to 86% of all adults.[4] They are also more likely than the rest of the population to use social media. A 2018 report from GlobalWebIndex reveals that UK mums spend more than two hours on social media each day and manage an average of seven social media accounts.[5] UK mothers are far more likely to spend time on social media than mothers in France, Germany and Spain, according to a Kantar report.[6] Like Australian mothers, they favour

1 www.nielsen.com/us/en/insights/reports/2018/from-consumers-to-creators.html
2 talktomums.co.uk/insights/
3 www.creativebrief.com/bite/what-mums-want
4 www.marketingweek.com/2014/04/10/the-five-myths-of-marketing-to-mums/
5 mobilemarketingmagazine.com/uk-mothers-social-media-millennial-money-savvy-globalwebindex
6 uk.kantar.com/media/668931/globaltgidispatches18_uk.pdf

Facebook significantly more than Instagram, and are likely to check their social media accounts as soon as they wake each morning. Social media is used by UK mothers to research products and find recommendations. The majority are part of closed Facebook groups just for mums, and this is where they often find out about other mothers' experiences with brands. It's their shortcut to finding genuine information about a product or service.

Work, judgement and guilt

There has been a significant rise in the number of women in the workforce post childbirth in the UK. Just shy of five million UK mothers work, up by more than one million over the past 20 years. Yet the British population aren't especially supportive of this. A British study of social attitudes found only 7% of British people believed UK mothers with kids aged under five years old should be working fulltime.[1] This judgement stings, and breeds guilt for mothers. And it's not surprising that with deep cultural attitudes such as this, there has been low numbers of dads staying home in the UK. Added to this strong judgement, these women are often stressed and time poor – an NUK survey revealed 69% of UK mothers worry they haven't got their work/life balance right.[2]

There is a great opportunity for a brand to support UK new mothers and take a stand to eradicate this judgemental attitude and assist them to find greater balance.

Changing shopping behaviours

A 2017 'Talk to Mums' survey of 2500 UK mums found that 50% had changed the way they shopped in the previous 12 months.[3] The survey noted a significant increase in online shopping by women

---

1 www.refinery29.com/en-gb/2018/07/204024/working-mothers
2 www.independent.co.uk/life-style/post-working-mum-adele-barbaro-real-mumma-facebook-office-difficulties-a8323691.html
3 talktomums.co.uk/women-shopping-habits-changing/

aged in their 30s, and a moderate increase in online shopping for women in their 40s. These are typically the years when women are child rearing, and given the increase in female workforce participation rates, it's not surprising they are turning to online shopping as they value convenience.

This provides complexity for grocery brands; how do they communicate new product offerings to mothers who order their groceries online all the time? Online mum forums provide an effective way to reach mothers about new product offerings, as well as communicating sampling options. Research shows that mums like to minimise their risk of purchase, and feel more likely to buy a product they've had the opportunity to try first.

Teenagers: the gateway to mum

A study by Mumsnet and Saatchi & Saatchi from 2016 provides great insights into UK mothers.[1] The 'Stop Faking It' report found that there are a total of 66 different identities mums associated with, which ranged from 'Mums with Menopause' through to 'Mums with Allergies', and everything in between. The report found the majority of UK mums identified with six different identities, highlighting the complex nature of being a mother. The two most common identities were 'Mums who Breastfed' and 'Mums who had Natural Births', each representing 5.7 million UK mothers. The next largest identities were 'Mums with a Child in Secondary School' and 'Mums with Teenagers', both representing 5.5 million mums across the UK.

These women are subtly but powerfully influenced by their teenagers in the categories of fashion, entertainment and lifestyle. To understand more about teenagers' influence on their mothers' spending, I spoke with Larissa Vince, Managing Director, Saatchi & Saatchi, London:

---

1 www.mumsnet.com/pdf/mumstock-2016-saatchi-research.pdf

'Teens are a big influence on their mothers' purchasing behaviour. This might be because women in their 40s and 50s no longer consider themselves old, and in fact like to keep up with trends as much as their kids do. We found that mothers are shopping in new places, both on the high street and online, and are trying new products based on their teens' recommendations. Marketers could do well to consider how they can use this important influencer group as part of their strategy.'

As the mother of two teenagers in Australia, I find all the best holiday adventures, places to eat and things to do via my 16-year-old daughter. She knows exactly where to go when I want to buy a pair of jeans, enjoy a chai or need a great new café to meet with a client. And I never would have discovered eyebrow mascara had my teenager not taken me beauty shopping. She understands my requirements and preferences, providing me with a powerful short-cut, saving me valuable time, and delivering against my needs. Why can't brands understand me like this? Teenagers could be a brand's secret weapon in influencing mums in the UK. They are willing to invest significant amounts of time in product discovery, something mums just don't have time for. Instead, mums have developed a series of shortcuts to help them accelerate through a purchase pathway. Whether it's accessing the information they need from a closed Facebook group, reading testimonials on a review site, or speaking to their teenager or other mums, they have a series of mechanisms they go to in order to find information quickly and efficiently. Brands wanting to get onto mum's shortlist need to be thinking about how they might be tapping into and influencing these shortcut methods.

The 'Stop Faking It' report is powerful as it provides deep insights into the true identities of UK mothers, and I highly recommend brands seek it out to understand UK mothers in greater depth.

Chapter 5: The geographic opportunities in the mum market

- Chinese mothers make 90% of the purchase decisions related to the child, making the mum market very attractive.

- India increasingly represents a highly attractive market for companies looking for significant growth.

- Australian brands are well positioned to service the boundless potential that exists in servicing Indonesian mothers, however they must have a local partner or engage a local distributor to sell into this market.

- There are 85 million mothers in the US who are responsible for US$2.4 trillion in spending annually.

- Mothers living in the UK are powerful and influential consumers, responsible for £205 billion in spending every year.

KEY POINTS

CHAPTER 6

INDUSTRY OPPORTUNITIES IN THE MUM MARKET

Travel, automotive, financial services and healthcare are four industries where there are numerous fantastic growth opportunities on offer. I'm a big believer that we can all learn a great deal and be inspired by things happening outside of our own industry, so if you don't operate in these industries you will still get something out of reading this chapter that will help you boost profits and grow your business.

Mums and travel

According to the World Travel and Tourism Council, global travel and tourism were worth US$7.6 trillion in 2016, and this is expected to grow to US$12 trillion by 2028. It is one of the fastest growing industries around the world, and accounts for 10% of global GDP. Take those numbers in; they are *huge*. Yet, the industry is not without challenges. The path to purchase is extremely long and complex.

Expedia Group Media Solutions research highlights that at least 50% of travellers are undecided on a destination and will make approximately 140 visits to travel websites before making a booking.[1] So, who makes the travel decisions, and how do you fast track the path to making a booking?

The huge impact of democratic parenting

It seems Millennial parents' egalitarian approach to parenting is shaking up the travel industry as they allow their children to have a greater influence than in past generations.

Expedia Group Media Solutions, the travel marketing platform of Expedia Group, recently released a report titled 'Generation Alpha & Family Travel Trends' which highlighted how the world's

---

1   https://info.advertising.expedia.com/multi-national-travel-trends-in-the-tourism-industry/

youngest generation, those born in 2010 and after (Generation Alpha), are influencing the global family travel market. In their quantitative study, they received more than 9000 adult responses across nine countries: Australia, Brazil, Canada, China, Germany, Japan, Mexico, the UK and the US. Each respondent had booked online travel in the past year and also was a parent or grandparent of a child born in 2010 or later. The Expedia Group Media Solutions research provides rich insights for any brand leader associated with the travel industry, and supports my own research that children have a growing influence in family travel decisions.

Expedia Group Media Solutions revealed that adults with Generation Alpha children are typically travelling more than three times a year, whether that be on a business trip, family holiday or kids-free break. When it comes to family holidays, adults still make the final travel choice, however kids do get a say. In fact, 80% said they frequently talked about travel with their Generation Alpha kids, and 60% of the family travel ideas came from both adults and kids. Their report reveals that nearly 9 out of 10 adults say planning a trip together can be fun for the entire family.

To understand the influence of kids on family travel more deeply, I reached out to Wendy Olson Killion, Vice President of business development at Expedia Group Media Solutions, who shared with me:

'Young children are already influencing their parents and family decisions, and that includes travel. Kids are growing up with tablets and smartphones and have more access to multiple sources of content – including online and TV – exposing them to new locations, information and inspiration for travel. As a mother of two kids under the age of 10, I witness daily the impact digital content has on them and their desire to explore new places and share experiences, in not only our backyard,

but the world. My kids have discovered new places in our city that are now regular hangouts. They already have a bucket list with many international destinations, as well as "playtoriums" one hour away, influencing both our short- and long-haul travel with their discoveries.

'The process of trip planning has evolved into a family affair, with the entire family playing an active role – including even the youngest members of the household. This is true for more than 80% of travellers around the world. Travel ideas are increasingly coming from both children and adults, and more than half of parents and grandparents said that they are being exposed to both online and TV content, shown to them by Gen Alpha family members, which factors into and influences family trip planning.'

The typical family holiday for parents with Generation Alpha children was enjoyed over seven days within the country they lived in, and they were likely to either fly or drive to get there. Parents are actively seeking out relaxation and fun with their family, and the top concern in choosing a holiday was the ability to keep the family happy and entertained. Surprisingly, families had a strong preference for staying in hotels over resorts or staying with family and friends. This is great news for anyone in the hotel business, but I would challenge you to ask: how are you appealing to this market segment?

While there is no denying the strong influence of Generation Alpha on their parents' travel decisions, the influence of Generation Z children should also not be overlooked. Let me share my own story with you. As a mother of three Gen Zs, I took my family on a month-long holiday through the US in late 2017. I was speaking at a conference in the US, and I thought I could combine business and time with the family. Like most mothers, I was the key decision maker when it came to choosing which country to travel to, however the kids largely influenced which locations within America we visited. My children's destination choices can be attributed to a small collection of famous YouTubers and sporting heroes they follow. We went to Hawaii after my 14-year-old daughter watched Jay Alvarrez countless times on YouTube, along with 10 million others. She wanted to visit some of Hawaii's 'hidden' gems Jay showed off in his videos. We went to Los Angeles as my 10-year-old daughter followed another YouTuber at the time by the name of Jake Paul and his Team 10. And my 12-year-old son, who aspires to play college basketball, wanted to see his beloved LA Lakers play a pre-season game against the LA Clippers.

Kids' influence over family travel is growing in line with the changing approach to family life, which is more democratic than in previous generations. Kids' voices are heard and considered. Astute travel marketers are recognising this and are running dual campaigns that separately target mothers and children. Without question, YouTube is a very powerful but underutilised tool for travel marketers.

Millennial mothers are seeking culturally diverse destinations

Millennial mothers are also shaking up the family travel market. Not only do they give their children a greater say in the family holiday experience, they are also opting for more culturally diverse destinations. They want their children to experience a different slice of life as they raise them to become global citizens. Hence, they are more inclined to travel overseas than Generation X mothers. This represents another great opportunity for travel marketers who can demonstrate how their destinations can provide unique experiences and diverse family offerings.

Wendy Olson Killion from Expedia Group Media Solutions shares:

'While Millennials may be having babies, these parents don't hesitate to travel with their kids. In fact, more than 60% of Millennial parents are traveling with kids under the age of five. Millennial parents are traveling with their families the same way they traveled without kids. This younger generation are the most likely to travel internationally and seek adventure. Just like their kids, they aren't looking for a watered-down, kid-friendly version of apps, content or experiences. Brands should be aware of this and focus on creating universal devices and experiences that everyone can use or enjoy, but that come with scalable safety features.'

Mums want flexible payment offerings

Two companies in Australia showing a clear understanding of the Millennial parent are Jetstar, a discount airline, and Afterpay, a 'buy now, pay later' provider. In late 2017 they announced flexible payment offerings for domestic fares within Australia. This was later expanded to include international flights, allowing Jetstar to see a significant lift in their Asian routes as Millennial families look for culturally diverse holiday opportunities as they seek to walk a less travelled road. With Afterpay now offered in the US and soon to launch in the UK, I expect the opportunity within the travel sector to be heightened.

Mums' trips

I'm seeing strong growth in girls' getaways where mums take a break from the rigours of family life to reconnect with girlfriends, recharge and relax from some of the responsibilities they juggle on a daily basis. The focus is on fun and relaxation. My Facebook newsfeed is filled with groups of female friends who are away on

159

their annual 'girls' trip' away. This trend is more pronounced in countries where there is longer annual leave provided by employers.

Solo mum travel

With the explosion in the health and wellness sector, mums are starting to reprioritise their own health needs and we are seeing wellness retreats becoming extremely popular, particularly among Generation X mothers. Mums are investing in self-care in record numbers, realising that if they are not at peak performance, their family will suffer. This is leading to the creation of solo travel for mums.

Let me share a story with you. Ros is an Australian single mother of two boys in her 40s. She works fulltime in the health sector, and takes off for at least one week every two years to attend a wellness program overseas. This break is designed to give her the space she needs to nurture her body and mind, set goals, and prepare for the road ahead. She said:

'Being a mother, but particularly a single mum, at times it feels like I have decision making burn out. Also working in the health sector, I know how important it is to invest in prevention, particularly for women in their 40s who are physically and mentally under a lot of pressure, especially when women experience some mental health conditions at higher rates than men.

'Today there are many retreats that are designed for solo travellers and particularly for women, and therefore solo travelling isn't as daunting as it used to be. Many of the women I've travelled with have taken this opportunity to reset a career pathway, to travel with a girlfriend, mother or sister, and to come up for air, invest in themselves and find their balance again.'

Mum business travel

Mothers are an untapped segment within the business travel market. There is scope for great improvement in catering for the growing number of mothers who are travelling for work. When booking accommodation, they are looking at the details, those little personalised touches that demonstrate a deep understanding of their needs and show that the hotel cares. They want high-quality bathroom products (including good toilet paper). They are attracted to hotels that can supply them with quality hairdryers and hair straighteners. They often don't want to dine alone in the hotel restaurant, nor do they want a heavy breakfast included. Ideally, they want to have much healthier options available to them to be delivered to their room, and easy access to a gym or a pilates or yoga class.

Intergenerational and 'skip gen' travel

An increasing travel trend is grandparents accompanying the family on large family holidays. More recently, though, we've seen grandparents travelling with their grandchildren *without* the parents. Known as 'skip gen' travel, it represents an enormous opportunity for travel brands.

Research by AARP – the world's largest not-for-profit membership-based community of people aged over 50 – reveals:

- 32% of US grandparents surveyed had taken a 'skip gen' trip with their grandchildren

- 15% of Baby Boomer grandparents surveyed were planning a 'skip gen' holiday in 2019

- 61% were interested in taking a 'skip gen' trip.[1]

This provides a great opportunity for grandparents to enjoy their role as historian and teacher on these holidays. The research also found that it's typical for grandparents to pay for 'skip gen' travel.

---

1 www.aarp.org/travel/vacation-ideas/family/info-2019/skip-generation-travel.html?intcmp=AE-HP-BB-LL4

I spoke with Patty David, Director of Consumer Insights at AARP to better understand this trend. He sees benefits for all generations of the family:

> 'Grandmothers desire a deeper connection with their grandchildren and distance is a challenge. Some are overcoming that challenge by taking their grandchildren on vacation without the parents. It's a win-win situation. Grandma gets to create a deeper bond and mom gets a much needed break.'

There's a similar trend being seen in the UK. In 2018 Disney on Ice commissioned a study to celebrate grandparents and found that one in five grandparents had taken their grandchildren on a holiday without mum and dad.[1]

Single-parent travel

There is enormous scope to tap into the growing solo mum segment and cater for their travel needs. Rather than having a pricing model for two adults, travel businesses can advertise pricing for a single adult and their children.

Gen Z travel

As the next generation of mothers comes through, travel brands will need to look at how they can assist Generation Z families to recuperate from the busyness of their lives and enjoy a digital detox. They will need to look at how they can accommodate family and solo holidays that allow them to seek out the meaning in life and support their spiritual pursuits. Their needs will see a distinct shift from the Millennial families who seek out Instagram-worthy holiday destinations.

---

1 www.independent.co.uk/news/uk/home-news/grandparents-technology-grandchildren-learning-social-media-a8520731.html

Brand considerations

Wendy Olson Killion shares her views and recommendations for travel brands:

'As digital marketing evolves, brands are navigating a travel landscape that is more crowded than ever before. Consumers are inundated with content from all directions and cutting through that can be a challenge for brands, especially when you don't know your audience. If you're marketing to moms, whether in the travel industry or elsewhere, personalisation is key. If you think all moms are the same, and don't know their mindsets or what inspires them, you won't be able to match them with the right message, at the right time, and on the right channel.

'Marketers are getting smarter about this from using data and strategic targeting, as the more you know about both your brand and your target audience, the more empowered you are to deliver creative, engaging and relevant experiences. When marketing travel to moms, or parents in general, we need to understand not only what inspires them personally when planning trips, but also the outside factors influencing their decision making. Are parents prioritising convenience or lowest price when selecting transportation and accommodations for family trips? Are they primarily looking for the best deal and value or is it about keeping their family entertained and happy? Are they the sole decision makers?'

Mums and cars

As a marketer I am fascinated by how automotive brands communicate with mothers. As a largely male-led working environment, I'm deeply concerned with the lack of understanding about mothers. At Marketing to Mums, I invest a great deal of research into the significant dissatisfaction among mothers with the automotive industry, and believe there is much work to be done. In a time when new car sales are slowing around the world, there exist some of the greatest opportunities to stand out as an automotive brand and better cater for the wants of mothers and their families.

A strong level of dissatisfaction

In 2018 Marketing to Mums undertook a study into what Australian mothers want from automotive brands. We surveyed 952 mothers to identify how they felt automotive brands were performing and how they could better cater for their needs. The results paint a picture of great opportunity, with 71% of mothers surveyed saying that automotive brands didn't understand them. To put this in some perspective, we asked 1800 Australian mothers whether they felt advertisers understood them in 2016: in this survey 63% of respondents felt brands and advertisers didn't understand them. So, there is a stronger level of dissatisfaction with the automotive sector, and this represents greater scope for growth. Automotive brands willing to invest in deeply understanding the wants of Australian mothers can reap great financial rewards.

Mums are the key decision makers

Dads might be coming into the dealership, but it's mums who are making the purchase decisions. In our research, 79% of mums identified themselves as being the key decision maker when it came to buying a car, and they were making this decision well before they ever set foot in a dealership. They were seeking the opinions of other mothers online, speaking with friends, and checking out the cars of other women at childcare and primary school.

The opportunity is *now*

The opportunity to find growth is immediate in the automotive sector. In our Marketing to Mums research, 68% of respondents stated they were in the market to buy a new car within the next three years.

What do automotive brands do wrong?

The top three mistakes mums feel automotive brands are making from our research are:

1. They treat mums like they are stupid.

2. They push their sales message too hard.

3. They stereotype mums.

Wondering if this was just an Australian viewpoint, I asked Mike Johnstone, Marketing Strategy Director from Volvo Cars UK, about what he thought the automotive industry was getting wrong:

> *'If I was to be critical, I think I would say it is not truly under-standing them as an audience to engage with. Often marketing in automotive can be very product focused with less concern over the target consumer's needs and wants. Sometimes we lead with product features first in communication without considering how relevant these are to our consumer. This is something that then creates homogeneous campaigns that don't truly appeal to any segment well. Naturally, mums are wise to this and can be alienated when they realise that their true needs aren't being fully considered within a piece of marketing communication. A better understanding of mums' needs – practical and emotional – is needed when communicating with them.'*

So, what *do* mums want?

As part of our Marketing to Mums research, we asked mums what they wanted from automotive marketers. Here's what they said:

> *'Stop selling to me like I'm defined by being a mum. My car is an extension of my identity (like my clothes) and I'd like that*

165

to be a good-looking, even sexy one – that is infinitely practical and gets the job done. These two factors seem to be mutually exclusive in car design. Sexy cars seem to be aimed at men whereas women get the school-run mobile. It's not only young, child-free women who get to be glam, so give me the car that reflects who I am. It needs the useful features and space for an actual life, as well as looking sexy and being fun to drive.'

'Target professional women. So much lifestyle imagery is about weekends and holidays and soccer practice.'

'What about trialling?! A test drive isn't really enough to really understand the needs of the family. It's like a house and you need to think about the ongoing needs of the family.'

'Females still allude to the need to bring a male car shopping with them so they don't get treated like an idiot or ripped off. This is shameful, particularly with the rise of independent and single parents who deserve equal treatment.'

It's become very evident that the way cars are designed is not meeting mums' needs. Our Marketing to Mums research identified eight significant product design features that mothers feel are currently lacking in the choice of cars. I was surprised by the simplicity of some of the design needs they felt were lacking with one of the top three desired new design features mums were asking for was somewhere to put her handbag. I believe involving mothers in the product design process would deliver a clear point of difference for an automotive brand in a highly competitive industry.

Where are they doing their research?

Mums are often avoiding going to the dealership to undertake their research, citing it is an 'unpleasant experience' and a 'sexist environment'. Most mothers are undertaking their research online; the dealership is reserved for the test drive and sales negotiation.

As a marketer and mother, I'm a member of a large number of closed Facebook groups, and I frequently observe mothers posting questions about the best seven-seater car for their family within a certain budget. Within hours, hundreds of women have responded, sharing their experiences and views on what is the best car and best value for money in a particular category. Mothers can very quickly refine their search through these groups. They also quickly discover what cars to avoid, as mums are quick to share their poor experiences also. While some countries are reporting a slow down in the use of Facebook among mothers, we are still seeing Facebook groups as being a key research base for most mothers. In fact, our Marketing to Mums research in Australia has seen an increase in mothers belonging to closed Facebook groups just for mums, from 66% to 80% over the three years to 2019.

When they arrive at a dealership, expect them to be very well researched, having a shortlist of no more than two cars and being very close to making a purchase decision. The challenge for most automotive marketers is therefore understanding how to influence mothers much earlier in the customer journey.

Environmental concerns

Increasingly we are seeing environmental concerns being a key part of mums' consideration set when purchasing a car. This view was echoed by Mike Johnstone from Volvo Cars UK:

'We are seeing an increasing amount of concern over environmental matters. This is something we are acutely aware of – ingrained within the DNA of our business since its inception is a desire to ensure that we minimise our environmental impact in everything we do. This isn't an opportunity per se, but a trend that we monitor and feel passionately about; as do parents.'

What's working?

In reviewing automotive advertising targeting women from around the world, I see Volvo as leading the way. The work they are doing to challenge existing automotive advertising to mothers is providing significant rewards. In 2018 they achieved a record-breaking number of awards including World Car of the Year and European Car of the Year[1], with global sales of 642,253 cars across 100 countries.[2] They are highly innovative. They invest heavily in research to deeply understand the customer. This customer-centric approach is delivering great dividends.

The 'Moments' campaign launched by Volvo to promote the XC60 in 2017 is a great example of an automotive commercial that deeply resonates with mothers. It's a highly emotive story of a little girl walking to her first day of school. She talks about all the adventures she plans to have in her life as she grows into an adult. All of this is risked when she steps onto the road in front of a distracted driver – who happens to be driving a Volvo XC60. The safety features of the Volvo prevent an accident. The audience breathes a great sigh of relief as the little girl carries on to school and is free to enjoy her future adventures in life. It's a high-impact commercial told in a very loving manner. (It was after seeing this campaign that I reached out to speak to Mike Johnstone from Volvo Cars UK to talk about it on Marketing to Mums – the Podcast.)

Video reviews represent another medium that is working particularly well in allowing women to understand the features of a car. They are far more receptive if a review is carried out by another mother who understands the key things mums are looking for, such as: will my pusher and the grocery shopping fit in the back seat?

---

1   https://www.media.volvocars.com/uk/en-gb/media/pressreleases/247432/volvo-car-uk-celebrates-stunning-record-awards-success-in-2018

2   www.media.volvocars.com/uk/en-gb/media/pressreleases/252083/volvo-cars-reports-74-per-cent-global-sales-growth-in-april

And can three car seats fit across the back seat? Longer videos are performing well.

What can your company do?

If automotive brands continue their current strategies, which mums report make them feel like they are stupid, mothers will continue to do their research behind closed doors, not involving the brand, and companies lose control.

Mothers in this segment are highly influenced by reviews, ratings and testimonials. In our Marketing to Mums research, 67% of Australian mothers said reviews, ratings and testimonials have the greatest influence when purchasing a car. This is much higher than in other industry categories. So, if you don't have a testimonial strategy yet, it might be time to give it consideration.

Understanding key trigger points for purchasing a new family car is important. Lots of work is required in cultivating relationships with women prior to them reaching certain life stages. Many women consider purchasing a family car some time before they fall pregnant. Additionally, mums are often triggered into considering a new seven-seater vehicle when they get pregnant with their third child.

Rewards abound in the automotive industry for brands willing to invest time and resources in better understanding this powerful and influential consumer segment. Utilising real customers who are mums in advertising is another opportunity.

Mums and financial services

Mothers seem largely overlooked when it comes to financial services. Kantar's 'Winning Over Women' report published in 2018 reveals that US financial services are losing out on US$782 billion in investible assets.[1] Despite 126 million American women controlling 51% of personal wealth, the Kantar report uncovered that financial services advertising dollars were 13 times more likely to be skewed to male media outlets than female. Seems like a big, attractive opportunity for operators within the financial services industry is going unnoticed.

Lack of trust and loyalty

Financial institutions are characterised by a lack of trust and loyalty across the globe. In Australia, this has been exacerbated by the recent Banking Royal Commission, which exposed widespread unscrupulous and sometimes fraudulent activity. Rather than going to banks or financial advisors for money advice, we see Millennial women turning to their mums.

Research by Facebook for Business in Australia has found that Millennials are far more likely than other generations to bank with multiple financial institutions. It seems there's a similar story in the US, with 31% of Americans having hardly any confidence in their financial institutions and their leaders.[2]

Mums and financial stress

In our 2019 Marketing to Mums survey of 656 Australian mothers, we asked them what was the biggest worry in their life right now. Overwhelming mothers are feeling financial stress, with 34% identifying that not having enough money was their biggest worry, significantly higher than any other response. When we ran the same study three years earlier, financial stress polled in a much lower position, with the health and safety of their children being their primary concern.

---

1 www.marketwatch.com/story/ignoring-women-is-costing-us-financial-service-companies-almost-800-billion-2018-12-05
2 www.apnews.com/293fb649770e4b0d89a6c69fe8c33897

Financial stress can heighten during particular times of the year, such as Christmas and other holidays, and during tax time. A Forbes article by Christine Michel Carter cited an H&R Block study which found that 42% of mothers feel overwhelmed during tax season.[1] This figure was primarily driven by the thought of owing money, and also having to gather tax documents to complete the tax return. There exists a clear opportunity for financial services organisations to better support mothers and their families.

Accessibility, convenience and personalisation

I've spoken with many mothers who feel ignored, even alienated, by the financial services sector. They don't feel represented by brands, and feel companies are slow to recognise the enormous opportunity they know they represent. The Editions Financial 'The Gender Lens' report identifies that women are expected to more than double their wealth between 2010 and 2020.[2] Yet, women across the globe feel misunderstood by their financial advisor; 86% of women in Hong Kong feel their financial advisor doesn't understand them. Women in the UK don't fare much better, polling at 73%, while the US achieved 44%. Opportunities clearly abound across the globe in deeply understanding their needs and requirements.

It's become clear that women seek out more long-term returns on their investments. They want to do more detailed research, and they have different investment priorities to men, notably wanting to leave a legacy for the family. Mums are also calling for financial providers to better cater to their needs as business owners. In Australia, women are entering business at almost three times the rate of men (and have been for the past decade), yet they feel ignored.

---

1 www.forbes.com/sites/christinecarter/2019/03/05/more-than-40-of-working-moms-feel-overwhelmed-during-tax-season/#2afae3774cfe
2 www.editionsfinancial.com/wp/wp-content/uploads/2018/09/EF4826-HNW-12pp-brochure-S12-PRINT-crops-NEW.pdf

One mother said:

'Cater for the huge number of mums in small business or self-employed. Despite the talk, there is just not enough support or interest from the banks for those in non-traditional work roles.'

On a more practical level, mums are calling for greater convenience. They want to avoid the need to go into branches or banking centres, and would prefer to have simple, efficient online options, as this mum shares:

'Be more accessible in terms of your opening hours or bring everything online. Between my kids and my business, I've found it really hard when I needed to get to the bank just to present my driver's licence. The bank in question was open 9:30am to 4pm, Monday to Friday, and the closest is 40 minutes from my home or office.'

Millennial mothers are seeking a mobile-first experience that delivers personalisation and utility. It's imperative that your brand offers services they can access each day on the go. Banking apps with payment gateways are a favourite for their cashless living. They are also happy to provide more personal details if it will result in a more personalised service.

To help understand where the industry might be going wrong, I spoke with a senior marketer from a global financial institution. We had met at a conference where I presented to a large group of senior financial services women. Her role had a focus on building diversity in financial services, so I was keen to understand her view on what the industry is getting wrong:

'The biggest mistake financial services organisations make in marketing to mothers is that we generalise too much – whether it is age, income bracket or interests. And also, we tend to retrofit what we are trying to sell to what we determine mothers are

interested in. We all know that we should be looking at clients or potential clients and working to solve the problems they have with a tailored solution but most of us don't do that.'

'I am a great believer in true diversity with particular focus on diversity of thought. I think we need to talk to people – not focus groups of customers, but more random groups to find what their priorities are and then try and figure out what we can offer them as ways to reach those priorities. We need groups working in house who have experience in other industries outside financial services and we need to take risks in differentiating ourselves properly from our competition.'

Understanding women's issues

I believe success for financial services brands will require them to have a deep understanding of the issues mothers face. These vary by priority based on a woman's stage of life or circumstances. Critical concerns that financial services companies could look to champion include:

- **A lack of superannuation:** An Australian report by Women and Money states that women have an average of 53% less superannuation at retirement than men. This is due to a range of issues, including the gender pay gap and career breaks for having children and caring for aging parents. Low superannuation levels are far more pronounced for single mothers.[1] In the UK, women aged 60 to 64 have accumulated only 25% of the pension amount that men have.[2] We have older women living in near poverty conditions, and women don't feel this issue is getting the air time it requires. Find a way to genuinely support them. Champion this issue for them.

---

1   www.womenandmoney.org.au/separation-and-divorce/
2   www.editionsfinancial.com/wp/wp-content/uploads/2018/09/EF4826-HNW-12pp-brochure-S12-PRINT-crops-NEW.pdf

- **The gender pay gap:** Around the world, women are facing lower pay than men. The gender pay gap is largest in the financial services sector, where it is 30%, almost double other industries. The World Economic Forum reported in the 2018 'Global Gender Gap Report' that we are 202 years away from closing the gap at our current rate of progress.[1] Until financial services organisations address the gender pay gap, they will continue to have a poor reputation and lack credibility among mothers. Women won't build trust with brands within the financial services sector until they address their own industry issues.

- **Financial empowerment:** Multiple reports point to women feeling less in control of their finances and financial futures than men. This is more pronounced among separated or divorced mothers. They are seeking someone to partner with to educate and empower them with their finances whom they feel they can trust.

The financial services sector is ripe for a disruptive force to genuinely understand and cater for the differing needs of mothers. Opportunities await those who choose to take a risk and do things differently.

The emerging Millennial opportunity

There is a significant shift occurring that will have far-reaching impacts on the bottom line of banks around the globe: Millennials are inheriting the world's wealth.[2] In Australia, Alex Boorman, Managing Director of Consulting at RFi Group, claimed in a recent report that 'the value of Millennials to the Australian

---

1   www.standard.co.uk/news/world/global-gender-pay-gap-on-track-to-close-in-202-years-according-to-the-world-economic-forum-a4021461.html
2   mumbrella.com.au/the-millennials-shall-inherit-the-earth-and-marketers-should-pay-attention-580161

financial institutions is expected to increase by almost 80% by 2025 whilst the value of Generation X and Baby Boomers will decline'.[1] They will represent the bulk of home loans and credit cards in Australia.

It seems there is a significant opportunity within the financial services sector to deeply understand the needs of Millennial mothers, as they are the CFO in the vast majority of households across the world. The Financial Brand report that 93% of women say they have significant influence over what financial services their family purchases.[2] Millennial mothers are demanding more digital tools to manage their finances. A 2018 GlobalWebIndex report of 1569 UK mothers found that they are 70% more likely to be purchasing financial products online.[3] They are also demanding greater transparency from their financial services partners.

This demand for digital product offerings and transparency will only increase with Generation Z mothers. Forbes reports that 70% of Gen Zs check their finances daily versus 61% of Millennials.[4]

Both generations value managing their finances. They see a healthy financial system as being important to their overall happiness. Financial providers need to explore how they can better cater for these expectations.

A financial services success story

MoneyLion is a US-based personal lending platform which provides a 'financial membership' rather than calling itself a bank. It's a clever distinction, and it highlights how they approach financial services differently – something that appeals to Millennial

1   https://s3-ap-southeast-1.amazonaws.com/fbb-brand-creative/anz-finserv-2019/
    Facebook+Connecting+With+Millennials+Retail+Banking+Report.pdf
2   thefinancialbrand.com/35365/marketing-financial-services-banking-to-women/
3   mobilemarketingmagazine.com/uk-mothers-social-media-millennial-money-savvy-
    globalwebindex
4   www.forbes.com/sites/madhvimavadiya/2019/05/26/fintech-is-putting-the-bank-of-mom-
    and-dad-out-of-business/#7ae370f79ab8

mothers. Launched in 2013 and now servicing more than four million Americans, MoneyLion is a great example of a business disrupting the banking sector. They aim to empower their members financially, and provide them with no-fee banking, fast loans, and a unique cash-back reward system. They have a very strong technical team and have embraced personalisation, using customer data to provide articles and content designed to assist them and deliver personalised money-saving recommendations.[1] They see a person's physical and financial health as being linked, and in early 2019 they launched an innovative financial tracker known as the Financial Heartbeat, allowing members to track the health of their finances at a glance.[2] This AI-powered tool is designed to grow their financial confidence and thereby improve their overall health and happiness. These features are well placed to appeal to mothers.

What I am particularly impressed with about MoneyLion is that they show a deep understanding of their customer and their changing needs, and are prepared to take risks to deliver something different to the market. They reach their largely mobile-first members via social media. New client acquisition has focused on Facebook, using video ads that are optimised for phone viewing to appeal to Millennials.[3] They also respond to emerging trends: after watching the growth of the gig economy, with people increasingly freelancing, they formed a partnership with Via to offer people working as freelancers a financial wellness program that provides seamless payments and educates them in financial literacy.[4] Given mums are entering the gig economy in droves, this product is well positioned for mum business owners. It's no surprise that MoneyLion's clientele are predominantly female. By addressing the

---

1   www.thedubs.com/5-us-banks-nailing-personalised-customer-service/
2   www.prnewswire.com/news-releases/moneylion-launches-the-financial-heartbeat----a-fitness-inspired-mobile-tracker-for-finances-300813742.html
3   www.facebook.com/business/success/moneylion
4   www.prnewswire.com/news-releases/moneylion-and-via-announce-new-financial-membership-program-300830462.html

biggest gender pay gap discrepancy of any industry, financial services brands will unlock the key to long-term growth in the mum market. This action will build credibility in a sector that has been discredited and has massive trust issues. There are also opportunities to re-examine financial services through a female lens and act differently to cater for a different set of needs.

Mums and healthcare

Mums are the key decision makers when it comes to healthcare. Consider them the Chief Medical Officer, the primary or joint health decision maker for their partner, children, extended family and loved ones, according to the 'Power of the Purse' report.[1] This report surveyed more than 9000 people across the US, UK, Brazil, Germany and Japan, and reveals that 94% of women make healthcare decisions for themselves and 94% of working mothers make healthcare decisions for others. They found women view healthcare more broadly than men, seeing good health as including emotional and spiritual wellbeing as well as being physically well. It's an important distinction which brands should be addressing in their business strategy, as it opens up options to incorporate many other disciplines, products and services in your offerings.

Lack of trust in healthcare

Brands operating within healthcare would be wise to address the growing mistrust that exists. The 'Power of the Purse' report found that 83% of women don't fully trust pharmaceutical companies, and 78% don't fully trust their insurance provider. Only 65% of women actually trust their doctors. Given the scope of influence mothers have over healthcare decisions, it's vital that brands address this as a priority. There is clearly a lack of confidence in the sector, and

---

1 www.talentinnovation.org/_private/assets/PopHealthcare_ExecSumm-CTI.pdf

healthcare operators would benefit from focusing on building trust through clear, detailed communications.

Information sourcing

Time-poor and technically savvy mothers are increasingly going online for their health information, and this is typically accessed via mobile. Pew Research identifies that women are significantly more likely to seek health information online than men.[1] Good search engine optimisation is therefore critical to ensure your brand's content is served up to your desired audience.

To find out more about how mothers search online for health information, as part of Marketing to Mums – the Podcast, I spoke with Hansa Bhargava, Senior Medical Director for WebMD, a health information website which has 76 million users each month. WebMD attracts many mothers to their website but is skewed towards Millennial mothers. They find the symptom checker tool – which helps them understand what steps to take next when there's a health issue – the most helpful. Typically, mothers are searching for information about colds, coughs, fevers and feeding, with 'what do I feed my child?' a top search. Hansa spoke to me about the importance of how healthcare brands should communicate with mothers. She cautions brands to ensure they reflect the different family structures that are much more common today. She recommends using conversational language which is free of jargon and lacks judgement. Information must be timely, and marketers must understand all 'mum moments' to deliver the right content at the time she needs it. She says coming across as being 'side by side' is a great way to speak and market to mothers in an equalised manner.

---

1   www.emarketer.com/Article/Women-More-Likely-Seek-Healthcare-Advice-Online/1009683

The rise of health apps

From pregnancy and baby tracking to managing physical activity levels, mums like to monitor their health and are increasingly using apps to facilitate this. Global downloads of medical apps is up 15% on the two years between 2016 and 2018, however we've seen enormous growth in countries such as Indonesia (up 110%), France (40%) and India (65%).[1] It seems clear that mothers are increasingly happy to share personal information via a health-related app if it provides value and utility.

Retail healthcare shopping

Research undertaken by Talk to Mums in the UK around women's changing shopping habits reveals that while UK mothers are enjoying the convenience of online shopping, they still seek out in-store shopping experiences. This is particularly the case in the healthcare category or for first-time mothers with a baby or toddler, who appreciate the opportunity to seek out expert opinions prior to purchase.[2]

'The Awakening'

I have observed mothers approaching menopause change their priorities in their life, and they reprioritise their own needs after years of putting their children's and family's needs first. This involves a strong focus on their own health as they seek to address nagging health concerns they have put off due to other family priorities. I call this 'The Awakening', and it sees them take greater control over the direction of their life. These women start to dream big again, wanting to actively plan for the next phase of their life, after their children finish school and their responsibilities diminish. They may take on a life coach or a personal trainer during this

---

1 www.appannie.com/en/insights/market-data/medical-apps-transform-patient-care/
2 talktomums.co.uk/women-shopping-habits-changing/

time – they are actively seeking change. It represents an important moment in a mother's life, and a significant opportunity for health brands to support her.

Healthcare growth areas

One of the exciting new developments in healthcare in recent times is the emergence of digital therapeutics. Still very much in its infancy, the category is set to grow to US$9 billion by 2025. Novita Healthcare is an Australian business offering digital therapy to address attention difficulties in children, suffered by a reported 136 million globally.[1] They have launched Tali Train, a TGA-approved five-week structured training program catering for children aged under eight years who have either ADHD or autism. The program is delivered via a series of games on a smartphone or tablet. It's incredibly attractive to parents as it's drug free, low cost, and can be specifically tailored for the child. To date they've had 1000 children participate in the program.

A health and wellness success story

All aspects of health and wellness are considered part of healthcare by mothers. They don't segment healthcare like most in the industry. They see it far more broadly. It's important that health marketers accommodate this view, and don't stick to the traditional structure. Understanding a mother's mindset is key to success.

There is enormous scope for growth in healthcare offering ingestibles, supplements and beauty drinks. Katerina Schneider started Ritual, a subscription-based vitamin company, after finding out she was pregnant and discovering most products had ingredients she found questionable. Being concerned about what she was putting into her body, Katerina developed vitamins that are vegan certified, gluten and allergen free, non GMO, and free of synthetic

---

fillers. Launched in 2016, Ritual is transparent in everything they do, from product sourcing to being able to see through the vitamin capsule. It's been an incredibly well received formula, with Ritual attracting strong investor interest and selling well over one million bottles. Katerina is one of many success stories found in healthcare who is redefining the way healthcare is delivered to mothers.[1]

---

1   monocle.com/radio/shows/the-entrepreneurs/393/

Chapter 6: Industry opportunities in the mum market

- Millennial parents' egalitarian approach to parenting is shaking up the travel industry as they allow their children to have a greater influence than in past generations.

- In a time when new car sales are slowing around the world, there exists some of the greatest opportunities to stand out as an automotive brand and better cater for the wants of mothers and their families.

- Mums are an attractive opportunity for operators within the financial services industry, but this is going largely unnoticed.

- Mums are the key decision makers when it comes to healthcare. Consider them the Chief Medical Officer, the primary or joint health decision maker for their partner, children, extended family and loved ones.

KEY POINTS

CHAPTER 7

THE FUTURE
OF MARKETING
TO MUMS

What does the future hold for marketing to mums, and how do brands stay ahead of the often changing conditions? Does your company know what's around the corner? How does your brand currently measure against the success factors which will determine the next decade in this burgeoning market?

I've been able to identify eight success factors that brands must be aware of and take action on if they are to successfully drive growth and profits and secure market share gains over the next decade in this area. As well as using my own experience and research, I also sought out the thoughts of more than 20 brand leaders, market researchers and marketing specialists to get different perspectives on how marketing to mothers will evolve over the next 10 years.

Success factor #1: Strong brand purpose

Brands will need to engage mothers on more than just their features and benefits in the coming decade. The 2020s will be all around meaningful marketing which is underpinned by purpose, trust and relevance. It will be critical that brands get clear on their purpose, and this must include strong contribution back to the community and society.

Purpose will become increasingly important as Generation Z women become mothers. As Mita Mallick, Head of Diversity and Cross Cultural Marketing at Unilever North America, shares:

'In 10 years, more of Generation Z will become moms. They are our first true digital natives, connected from birth to technology. They are economically conservative having experienced the 2008 financial crisis and having experienced global instability. They are social activists and they will continue to use their collective voices to champion and support those brands that reflect their values. And they will challenge those brands who stand in opposition to what they believe.'

Brands without a clearly articulated and 'lived' purpose will be under great pressure. They will be forced to play a strong price game to find growth as mothers increasingly want brands to contribute to the healthy progression of society. Brand purpose can differentiate a brand by standing for something much greater than themselves.

Barbie represents an excellent case study of a brand that has successfully transformed itself to become relevant again and build trust by promoting their purpose to better reflect the views of modern mothers.

Barbie was launched in 1959 by working mother Ruth Handler, who wanted to inspire young girls to be anything they wanted to be. Barbie – with her curvaceous shape and blonde hair and blue eyes – was a hit, and one billion dolls have been sold across more than 150 countries. But by 2014, things were looking bleak. Barbie had lost relevance among the changing expectations and cultural views of modern mothers. Sales were in free fall. Barbie now typified an unrealistic body image and gender stereotype that no mother wanted to endorse or perpetuate.[1]

A radical transformation ensued. The company tapped into their purpose to inspire girls to be whatever they wished to be, and looked to reflect the cultural views of today's mothers. Mattel undertook extensive research, which revealed that 90% of mothers felt their daughters needed more positive role models. They listened deeply to mothers' views and took risks. This resulted in a greater diversity of options for Barbies. A total of 23 new Barbies were introduced into the range, which included women of colour, different hair colours, three different body shapes, and Barbies of all abilities. They also added career Barbies to the range.

Mattel also focused on developing much stronger relationships with mothers around the world. The focus was on connecting them to Barbie's purpose. To do this they embraced digital technologies,

---

1 www.chiefmarketer.com/barbies-journey-from-free-fall-to-sales-growth-cmo-juliana-chugg/

producing some award-winning YouTube videos. 'Imagine the Possibilities' went viral and has had more than 50 million views.

More recently, Mattel has embarked on an ambitious program to help young girls across the world dream big. The campaign is called 'Close the Dream Gap'. It was launched with a video of young girls telling us some disturbing statistics, such as from the age of five girls stop believing they can be an astronaut, president, or scientist. Close the Dream Gap resonates strongly with mothers, who love that Barbie is taking a stand and supporting them to help their girls dream big.

Speaking at the ANA Brand Activation Conference in the US in 2019, Lisa McKnight, SVP, Barbie and Global Head of Dolls at Mattel, said:

> *'The toy business is full of toys that peak quickly and then disappear. The purposeful brands, brands that engage with an idea that's bigger than products, can have staying power for generations. Today's consumer wants brands they can believe in.'*[1]

The changes to Barbie have proved a sales success, providing Mattel with their best sales results in five years and six consecutive quarters of growth.

Mattel have also partnered with Mercedes-Benz. In 2019 they are sharing the story of Ewy Rosqvist, the first female to win a Grand Prix race. Matchbox have created a replica of Ewy's Mercedes-Benz, which they are gifting to thousands of first-grade girls, and they are sharing Ewy's story to help reshape their thinking that girls can do anything.

Purpose will become paramount to securing brand growth in the 2020s as mothers become more conscious shoppers. Your brand purpose has the capacity to set you apart from your competitors

---

1 www.chiefmarketer.com/barbie-takes-on-closing-the-dream-gap-for-girls/

and drive strong relationships with mothers. It can drive growth and product or service differentiation and position your brand in the marketplace. But success will only be derived if your message is deemed authentic and is embedded deeply in the culture and workings of your organisation. Like fake reviews, mothers will sniff out inauthenticity in an instant. You must review your brand and its greater purpose for mums and society if you are going to get ahead with mums.

Success factor #2: Rapid growth in femtech

There is a significant shift taking place in the business world right now: women are using technology to solve real pain points they have experienced for years and that up until now have been largely ignored by brands. Known as 'femtech', it involves using technology to create innovative new products and services which focus on women's health. It includes:

- wearable technology products
- apps to track fertility, periods and pregnancy
- sexual wellness and mental health services
- tampon alternatives.

This will impact women of all ages, across generations. Frost & Sullivan predict this market will grow to US$50 billion by 2025. As women's purchasing power increases, femtech will provide growing opportunities for brands and investors over the next decade and beyond.[1] It's attracting strong interest in investor circles, with US$1 billion in investments made since 2014. Femtech founders tend to be females who are seeking to address the previously ignored

---

1   venturebeat.com/2018/03/08/frost-sullivan-femtech-could-become-a-50-billion-market-by-2025/

health needs of women. They are redefining the healthcare category by approaching innovation through a female lens. These women are tackling previously taboo issues such as incontinence. Menopause is another area that is poorly catered for right now – I expect we will see some femtech solutions offered in the marketplace over the next decade, and we will see menopause going mainstream. This is all supported by Frost & Sullivan, who found that women are 75% more likely to use digital tools for healthcare than men.

The market is still very much in its infancy, with the majority of femtech businesses only launching in the past five years. It's an incredibly exciting time for women's health. I spoke to Marija Butkovic, CEO of Women of Wearables – the first global organisation aiming to support, connect and mentor women in wearable tech, fashion tech, health tech, Internet of Things (IoT) and VR/AR – who believes:

> 'Focusing on supporting and investing in the next generation of femtech businesses means not only the rise of women in this space. The whole industry will benefit from it because it finally won't be missing out on some potentially great businesses that are not only created by women, but for women. Half of the world's population is female so we definitely cannot be niche.'

A femtech success story is Elvie, a health technology company from the UK founded by Tania Boler. Elvie is a great example of a brand doing things differently by delivering innovative products catering for women's health. Their first product addressed incontinence, which affects twice as many women as men. It is a silicone Kegel exercise tracker worn internally and connected via Bluetooth to the Elvie app to measure and track pelvic floor muscle movements.

Elvie is also being richly rewarded by mothers with waitlists for their second product, a silent, tubeless, wearable breast pump which fits inside a nursing bra. The product syncs with and is controlled by a smartphone to monitor breast milk output, allowing a nursing mother to pump milk without anyone even being aware of it. Launched in October 2018, it is claimed to revolutionise breast-feeding for working mothers across the world.

Elvie caused a stir by doing things differently, a winning formula in my book. To support the new product launch they featured a catwalk model mum pumping in their finale to demonstrate that it can be done anywhere, anytime. Ahead of Mother's Day in 2019, they used large inflatable breasts to start a discussion about the stigma mothers felt around breastfeeding in public. It's this different approach, coupled with their innovation-led products, which has really attracted the interest of tech-first mums around the world.

I believe the rise of femtech and women in entrepreneurship and innovation will disrupt existing industries. Expect a significant rise in women launching innovative tech products for mothers, with new ways of dealing with long overlooked problems. Many brands would be wise to invest in some of these companies and learn from the female lens they apply.

Success factor #3: Understanding mums' moments

Critical to any brand's future growth and success with mums is better understanding mums' moments; communicating with her using the right channels, with the right language at the right time. This might sound elementary to some, however I am staggered by the lack of focus displayed by brands in understanding these moments and how they apply to their brand. The coming decade will see successful brands adopt a moment-based approach to their marketing. As Phillip Lynch, Vice President of Growth & Innovation at Johnson & Johnson Asia Pacific, shares:

'Brands need to be there at the right moment, and not at the wrong ones if they wish to be viewed as meaningful. Brands

*need to be authentic and relevant, with messages that
acknowledge how mum thinks and feels, and can demonstrate
how the brand fits in with her view of the world - in our case,
her parenting routines.'*

Technology and data services such as Foursquare will enable
marketers to better understand mums' journeys and allow an opportunity to be far more relevant and part of their lives. This will also
assist marketers to better understand the different personas mothers play every day, as Wendy Liebmann, founder of WSL Strategic
Retail, explains:

'The decade ahead will be much more personalised and
customised. The future will be all about recognising that she
may be a mom, but she's a lot of other things too - an executive,
a girlfriend; sometimes she's a Millennial mom and sometimes
she's a Boomer mom; sometimes she's a price-hunter, sometimes
a browser who will spend more because of the experience. One
of the biggest mistakes marketers make today is thinking a
mom is only one person. In the future, analytic data will enable
companies to more intimately understand who she is, when, and
customize the experience, products and solutions to her at that
moment. And that will be a real opportunity - and necessity.'

Wendy's company, WSL Strategic Retail, undertook research
titled 'Future Shop: A View to 2020', which revealed that 80% of
shoppers will get what they need wherever they happen to be. It's
a significant insight which Wendy believes is driven by the ubiq-
uity of choice today combined with families' desire to be efficient.
Shoppers no longer have a handful of places they shop in – there
is now enormous choice for accessing products and services as we
need them. Wendy believes marketers and retailers need to understand a mother's desire to use her time more efficiently. They must
identify her need states, so they can tap in at the right time and solve

her problem for her and build loyalty. She says that 'if you don't fine tune your understanding, then there are so many places she can shop for the same sort of stuff. There's a real risk you could lose her as she goes somewhere else.' Wendy recommends understanding her, her life stage and her life need at that moment. She pointed out a simple insight that most mothers don't know at 4pm what they are cooking for dinner and how a retailer could tap into this and provide her with an efficient solution at this particular time.[1] She cited an example of Walmart and Coke, who collaborated with a meal solution that they advertised via radio when many mothers were driving after picking up their kids from school at around that time. Recognition and deep understanding should also be focused on key life moments for mothers, such as:

- first day back at work after maternity leave

- first day of childcare for a child

- getting pregnant with the second or third child.

Successful brands will be able to identify a mum's life moments through a combination of customer journey mapping and research, and deliver personalised communications to support her. Unsuccessful brands will keep using today's techniques in the years ahead.

Success factor #4: Voice and visual search will dominate

Voice will transform the way mothers discover new brands over the next ten years. People are increasingly turning to voice searches and this will have a far-reaching impact on how mothers discover new brands and transact with businesses. Mums and their children are using vocal commands to conduct internet searches via voice

---

1 marketingtomums.com.au/podcast/ep14_wendy_liebmann_how_mums_shop/

technology. This is particularly so among new tech-first mothers with young children who prefers using vocal commands as she might not have her hands free to type her search.

The rise in voice search can be attributed to the growing trend for families to own a smart speaker, along with the increasing use of voice assistants such as Siri on the iPhone. One study claims smart speaker penetration is outperforming smartphones and tablets at a similar stage. Penetration doubled in 2018, and in 2019 shows no signs of slowing down.[1] China currently represents the largest market with a third of all volume, however penetration is higher in Germany, the US, France and the UK.[2] The Chinese market is very different from the rest of world due to the absence of Google and Amazon. Instead the Chinese market is dominated by Alibaba's Tmall Genie and Xiaomi's MiA AI smart speaker.[3] In the US, Edison Research reports that 34% of mothers have a smart speaker in the house, with the most popular being Amazon Alexa.[4]

In Australia, we recently conducted our 'Tech-first Mums' research where we surveyed 656 mothers, and we found that 23% own a smart speaker, with Google Home being the preferred option. Perhaps far more telling is that 13% of Australian mothers intend to purchase a smart speaker in 2019. It really is the year of voice technology. Word of mouth is driving this growth. I spoke with Kath Blackham, founder of Australia's first and only voice agency, VERSA, who believes:

'Voice is the biggest disruption in our industry since Apple introduced apps in 2007.'

'I think we will look back and view Voice as being as big as the start of the internet. It's a much greater paradigm shift

---

1 finance.yahoo.com/news/smart-speaker-sales-growing-faster-152339686.html
2 voicebot.ai/2018/08/16/china-is-driving-half-of-global-smart-speaker-growth/
3 voicebot.ai/2017/07/26/xiaomi-mi-ai-smart-speaker-takes-alibaba-tmall-genie-linglong-dingdong/
4 www.edisonresearch.com/moms-and-media-2019/

and brings us back to where communication started, people speaking to people. Voice is the new internet.

'I don't believe Voice will replace a full website however, it will act as the entry point for new information. It will be a place of discovery. Within ten years, I believe Voice will have taken over as the dominant start of a brand experience. It will be multi-modal where we use Voice to start the search and then seek things out on screen.

'In the future I believe AI will play a greater role in Voice. We will move beyond smart speakers and see voice integrated into our everyday products with a lot of natural language used.

'My advice to brands is that they get started now, to test and to learn. Brands have the opportunity to surprise and delight mums by being first to market and building something new and interesting. Given there are currently a few brands invested in voice, they have the opportunity to make some mistakes and learn, so when voice really takes off in the coming years they are well equipped and prepared to invest heavily in voice knowing that it will work successfully.'

The early adoption of the smart speaker by families will have a massive impact on the way we market to mothers in the next decade. Voice search results in a different type of search than we see in written form. It becomes less about keywords, as people search in questions adopting a conversational tone. What might have been '7 seater family SUV near me' might become 'What is the best 7 seater family SUV I can test drive?' It's an important distinction.

Grocery retailers have been fast to adapt to this trend. In early 2019, Walmart partnered with Google's smart home assistant to offer voice-activated shopping, allowing customers to order their groceries using voice instead of ordering via their mobile or desktop. In Australia, Woolworths is the first supermarket to utilise voice in this way, allowing customers to add to their shopping lists using voice commands.[1] It's likely this will be rapidly adopted by mums who are seeking greater convenience over the next decade.

Over the next decade voice has the capacity to transform mums' lives globally. If technology is able to overcome the current limitation of providing one search result and it can act as a vehicle for brand discovery, it will effectively act as mum's personal assistant, providing her with greater efficiency and convenience. Visual search doesn't get the same attention as voice right now, but it will have significant impact over the coming decade.

Visual search allows users to locate other items similar to an image they capture. For example, I can take a photo of a dress I like in a shop and an app can bring up similar dresses available for me to purchase. Visual search recognises both images and videos, and will really impact the way women shop in the future, particularly as our tech-first mothers grow in numbers. It will require brands to pay greater attention to image SEO, making it more important to use original images rather than relying on stock images.

Amazon and Pinterest are really leading the charge to develop visual search tools, but many other big brands are already exploring visual search capabilities, including Target (US), ASOS, eBay and Google. In 2018 Pinterest reported that more than 600 million visual searches were conducted each month using their Lens technology, their visual search tool, with fashion and homewares the categories of greatest interest. This was up 140% on 2017, and is only set to increase as the Lens technology becomes more sophisticated.[2] Last year they also partnered with Samsung so that visual search is now possible on all their recent smartphones.

Mothers are early adopters of technology. We've seen this time and again, and voice and visual search adoption will be no different.

---

1 www.insideretail.com.au/news/woolworths-gifts-voice-tech-to-online-shoppers-201906#daily

2 newsroom.pinterest.com/en/post/celebrating-one-year-of-pinterest-lens

Brands wanting to reach mothers will need to embrace these new search formats sooner rather than later. Don't delay.

Success factor #5: Experiential marketing

Experiential marketing, where a product or service is promoted through an experience, will become increasingly important and valuable in marketing to mothers in the coming decade. Despite all the advances in technology and growth in online sales, mums still seek out the human element. Real-life connections still count, and emotional connections will win no matter how much technology you have on your side. It doesn't matter the age of the mother; all generations are still valuing personal interaction with their favourite brands. Brands that miss this success factor risk being left behind.

Experiential marketing will allow brands to create unique, fun, memorable moments with mothers, which are lasting and more effective than many other traditional marketing efforts. Millennial and Generation Z mothers are increasingly seeking out unique experiences that provide them with talking points with their friends. Experiential marketing will go a long way in helping brands build closer, lasting relationships with mums. It also fosters customer loyalty and advocacy, as mothers are more likely to share their positive experience with the brand. They will share the story of the great event you created. It also helps brands demonstrate that they understand mothers, an important factor in winning them over. Lastly, it can be a great vehicle to show your brand purpose.

As an example, in Australia we've seen Birdsnest, a women's online fashion brand, create behind-the-scenes experiences where fans can tour the head office, meet with a stylist, purchase clothes and enjoy lunch.[1] And beauty lovers are still talking about MECCALAND, Australia's biggest beauty festival created by

---

1 www.insideretail.com.au/news/inside-the-nest-birdsnest-opens-its-doors-to-customers-201906

leading beauty retailer MECCA. Run over three days and featuring more than 40 global beauty brands, more than 15,000 devoted customers were able to secure limited-edition products before they were released to the public and gain access to global make-up artists, beauty influencers and beauty founders to learn new techniques and hear behind-the-scenes news. MECCALAND was an incredible success at facilitating stronger relationships with Millennial and Generation Z women in Australia. It's not limited to beauty and apparel either. We've seen the success of Luxury Escapes, an Australian travel company specialising in total package getaways to premium resorts across the world. They arrange meet ups overseas for their customers, where they put on drinks and socialise with them while they are on holiday. It has proven an excellent way for the organisation to stay connected with their customers and build relationships, and also understand what they want next. It seems an excellent vehicle to engage in informal market research.

In the US we are seeing experiential marketing play out in new ways. I was reading the Springwise newsletter recently and they have identified the merging of co-working spaces with retail.[1] Take Care is a wellness-oriented co-working space in Washington which offers wellness classes. It also has a beauty shop within the space so workers can enjoy treatments and purchase new products while at work. In the UK, Disney partnered with Tesco to create in-store 'teddy surgeries' to promote the second series of Doc McStuffin, about a six-year-old who heals bears and other toys.[2] Technology will increasingly feature in experiential marketing efforts. Both Artificial Reality (AR) and Virtual Reality (VR) can really enhance experiential marketing efforts and can be used to create more sensorial experiences for customers. As events become more sophisticated, I believe that not only will brands be able to successfully strengthen relationships but they will also use the

---

1 www.springwise.com/us-store-merges-retail-co-working-space-and-wellness
2 econsultancy.com/10-examples-experiential-marketing/

experiences to detail other product and service offerings in a more palatable way where people don't feel sold to, activating a significant sales opportunity also.

In a recent study, 77% of women said that a live demonstration or experience helped them understand a product.[1] That's a great opportunity. I encourage brands to investigate how they can utilise experiential marketing practices combined with a surprise and delight strategy to give your brand a competitive edge in the marketplace.

Success factor #6: The booming sharing economy

With Millennials and Generation Z owning less – coupled with the drive towards minimalism, sustainability and the desire to save time and money – we will see the share economy disrupt current market sectors and selling models in coming years.[2,3] For example, I believe we will see this trend disrupt high-value nursery items, with increased renting of top-line cots and other nursery products in coming years.

A Nielsen study showed that 68% of global consumers are open to sharing their possessions for financial gain.[4] The Asia-Pacific region is the most open to sharing, while Latin America, the Middle East and Africa are significantly more receptive than the US and Europe. Has your brand started preparing for how the sharing economy might disrupt your future strategy?

I spoke with Michelle Poris – Vice President at Smarty Pants, a leading youth and family research and consulting firm in the US – about the future growth in the sharing economy and how it will impact brands selling to mothers:

---

1 cdn.eventmarketer.com/wp-content/uploads/2016/01/EventTrack2015_Consumer.pdf
2 www.cognizant.com/perspectives/the-rapid-rise-of-the-sharing-economy-part1
3 www.asksmartypants.com/reports-subscriptions/it-takes-a-village
4 www.nielsen.com/au/en/press-releases/2014/global-consumers-embrace-the-share-economy/

'Consumers are increasingly comfortable with the sharing
economy, but ubiquitous peer-to-peer brands like Uber, WeWork,
and Airbnb represent only the tip of the potential iceberg. High
interest in share communities is seen globally, with Nielsen data
suggesting that consumers in developing regions like Asia-Pacific
and Latin America are even more open to participation. In fact,
China, Indonesia, Slovenia, Philippines, and Thailand report
the highest interest in share community products and services.
For Millennial moms, in particular, tapping into the sharing
economy for their parenting practices comes naturally, as they
are comfortable with the digital platforms that facilitate share
services and they are looking for ways to save time, money,
and environmental resources. Moms are turning to kid-friendly
rideshare companies (bringing kids to school, playdates, sports
practices, and more), kids' toy- and game-sharing companies, kids'
apparel sharing services, and childcare/babysitting co-ops. Other
emerging family-oriented share opportunities include dinner
co-ops/share programs and early childhood education co-ops.'

In Australia, we've seen the success of Shebah, a women-only
(and boys aged up to 12 years) ride-sharing platform that has only
female drivers. It's designed to help women feel safe and help manage the ever increasing number of pick-ups, drop-offs and sport
commitments most mums struggle to manage. Founded by mum of
four George McEncroe, Shebah recently broke records by raising
$3 million in a month-long Birchal crowd equity funding cam-
paign. A staggering 94% of the 2100 investors were women, again
highlighting the trend mentioned earlier in the book for women
wanting to support other women in business.[1] Later in 2019, we
will see the childcare industry in Australia disrupted with KidNest,
a parent-to-parent introductory platform designed to facilitate
an affordable, local and flexible alternative to childcare (and a

---

1   www.smartcompany.com.au/startupsmart/news/shebah-3-million-equity-crowdfunding/

company I play a Board Advisory role for). For a monthly subscription, registration on the KidNest digital platform enables parents to create or join a child-minding 'nest' in their neighbourhood that meets their unique needs and provides them with time to return to work, study, or just have some time out. With funding and trials already underway, expect KidNest to take on larger markets soon, including the US.

Brands are recognising this growing trend and are looking to launch new business models. One Dutch company called MUD Jeans allows customers to rent their jeans and after a year they can either keep them or return them, with all returned jeans being recycled. Each pair of jeans is made from 40% recycled jeans and 60% organic cotton. It's perfectly tapping into the growing trend among mothers for sustainable fashion. Tchibo, one of Germany's biggest retailers, in 2018 partnered with a children's clothing rental business to launch Tchibo Share.

Volvo foresaw the growth and disruption occurring through the sharing economy and has looked for ways to capitalise on this trend within the automotive sector. With the trend for younger people wanting to own less, they have introduced a subscription model on their XC40 model, which is likely to be extended in line with demand. As Generation Z become parents, I believe we will see this subscription model grow among other automotive brands.

The sharing economy and new renting and subscription models have great capacity to disrupt unsuspecting companies and industries. Be prepared and be proactive and challenge your current ways of thinking, and consider new delivery models that better meet the needs of mums. There are great gains to be made with the first-mover advantage.

Success factor #7: Being mother-centric

In researching for this book, I spoke with many brand leaders and it quickly became apparent that they feel success in marketing to mothers in the coming decade will require brands to have a very deep understanding of their niche segment of the mum market. It's very much a case of going back to basics for many brands and ensuring their strategy is mother-centric. Engage in fresh research to clearly identify your most profitable segment of the mum market and deeply understand their behaviours, motivations and expectations from your brand. This might appear obvious however I can't tell you how many times I see this overlooked.

Successful brands in the 2020s will be customer-led. They will stay closely connected to their buyers to be able to respond and adapt quickly to behavioural changes. As Mike Johnstone, Director of Marketing Strategy at Volvo Cars UK, shared:

> *'I think this segment – like many others – is becoming ever more savvy, with increasing awareness of brands and products through a multitude of digital channels. I think social media will play an increasingly important role – but less through traditional "influencers" and more through genuine word of mouth and customer advocacy. Brands need to ensure they truly understand their customers and deliver on their expectations in order to create the evangelists that will share stories and experiences which engage new customers. Being truly customer-led will be key; understanding what mothers really need and not treating them as an analogous whole will be essential for brands to prosper. The opportunities are massive.'*

It's a sentiment shared with experienced FMCG brand leader Bill Partyka. Bill has deep insights about mothers from his 20-plus years' experience working in the consumer foods industry with leading global brands, including Wyeth Nutrition, Healthy Choice and

General Mills, and now as President and Chief Executive Officer of Gerber Product Company. Leading the biggest baby food company in the world, I spoke to Bill about the customer-centric approach which has allowed Gerber to grow and adapt as mums' views have changed. Bill believes Gerber has been so successful since launching in the 1920s because they have always stayed very connected to their customers. Listening to mums' needs has enabled them to respond and stay relevant. They've found new trends emerging with the arrival of Millennial mothers, which has required them to focus on transparency, clear packaging, natural product offerings and freshness. They are always focused on the customer in everything they do.

Technology advancements will assist in leading a level of customer personalisation we haven't seen yet. As Jola Burnett, Vice President at GfK, explains:

> 'The future of marketing will be powered by digital technologies that boost customer experience and personalization. We are moving towards a-commerce (both augmented and AI driven) transactions. AI is already curating moms' choices (based on their unique needs, tastes and likes) – think Netflix or Amazon recommendations. AI-powered chat bots will take care of the mundane tasks for moms; for example, from booking appointments to putting together customized recipes. Chat bots will be extensions of brands, providing superb service and improving customer experience.'

Understanding that mums value convenience and efficiency and responding with technology that meets these requirements will be warmly received by mothers and assist in building loyalty. I recommend setting up a structure which enables your brand marketers and senior marketers to stay closely connected with your core customers, and that you put your most profitable segment of the mum market at the core of everything you do. This will yield deeper insights and understanding, and lead to a more effective and productive marketing strategy. It's these basics which other brands are not undertaking to the depth required where market share gains can be made.

Success factor #8: Facebook Libra will transform how mothers shop

In June 2019 Facebook announced that they will launch their cryptocurrency Libra, which will enable people to buy things or send money to people with very low, almost zero, fees. Set to launch in 2020, I believe Libra will change commerce and banking around the world as mothers embrace a new way to shop.

> *'I am extremely proud to represent Women's World Banking as a Founding Partner in the Libra Association. Libra has the potential to level the playing field for the 1.7 billion people who remain unbanked and excluded from formal financial services – over half of whom are women! This may be the pivotal moment in time when we look back and recognize we had the key that unlocked the door for billions of people!'*
>
> *Tom Jones, Executive Vice President & Chief Operating Officer, Women's World Banking*[1]

I believe Libra will change the game. Over the next decade, I see Libra being widely adopted by mothers across the globe. Mothers are early adopters of new technology; we've certainly seen this time and again with the smartphone, wearable technologies and smart speakers. The introduction of Libra, accessed via a digital wallet Calibra, will remove friction and increase the speed and convenience of online shopping, something mums increasingly value as they manage their time.

---

1   https://libra.org/en-US/media-press-news/

Mums love Facebook. In fact, in our 2019 Marketing to Mums survey we found that Facebook remains the preferred social media platform for mums of all ages in Australia. The privacy scandal where 50 million Facebook users had their personal data compromised has not impacted mums' use of Facebook. Throughout our Marketing to Mums research, use of Facebook has remained stable throughout the privacy breach issues. I certainly noticed there was a segment of mothers reconsidering their use of the platform, however this group reduced significantly once they realised the ease with which the platform allows them to stay connected with other mums, and they remain active on the platform. Additionally, many liked seeing the regulators stepping in to address the privacy breaches. It brought some comfort to them.

When I interviewed Melissa DeCesare, VP at Edison Research, for the Marketing to Mums podcast, she mentioned that, while they were not exploring privacy breaches, they did note that mothers' use of Facebook has remained healthy, contrasting to the general population where they'd seen a drop off of those using the platform.

Facebook Libra has surprised many with its level of privacy and data protection, and this will make mothers more comfortable using it. Financial data will be kept separate from social media data via Calibra. I was reading an article in TechCrunch which stated:

'Facebook's audacious bid to create a global digital currency that promotes financial inclusion for the unbanked actually has more privacy and decentralization built in than many expected.'[1]

Mums will be swayed by the heavy third-party support for Libra. Big brands such as eBay, Spotify, Mastercard, Visa, PayPal and Uber have been announced as founding members of Libra Association,

---

1   https://techcrunch.com/2019/06/18/facebook-libra/

the independent authority for the cryptocurrency. This will serve as strong endorsement for the payment service.

Initially, I see Libra proving popular among migrant mothers, looking to transfer money back home to family members without the high transaction fees. It will also perform strongly in developing countries where mothers may not have bank accounts. In developed countries I believe Generation X mums and older Millennial mums who dominate Facebook use will widely support Libra.

Facebook's entry into financial services is bold, and has the capacity to create enormous disruption and challenges for the financial sector. Whatever your view on Facebook is, the brand is certainly set to grow in power and dominance over the coming decade. I strongly recommend that brands watch the launch of Libra and Calibra closely and carefully consider their brand's involvement in allowing customers to pay using Libra.

Chapter 7: The future of marketing to mums

- The 2020s will be about meaningful marketing which is underpinned by purpose, trust and relevance. It will be critical that brands get clear on their purpose.

- Women are using technology to solve real pain points they have experienced for years and that up until now have been largely ignored by brands.

- Critical to any brand's future growth and success with mums is better understanding mums' moments; communicating with her using the right channels, with the right language at the right time.

- People are increasingly turning to voice searches, and this will have a far-reaching impact on how mothers discover new brands and transact with businesses.

- Experiential marketing, where a product or service is promoted through an experience, will become increasingly important and valuable in marketing to mothers in the coming decade.

- With Millennials and Generation Z owning less – coupled with the drive towards minimalism, sustainability and the desire to save time and money – the share economy will disrupt current market sectors and selling models in coming years.

- Successful brands in the 2020s will be customer-led. They will stay closely connected to their buyers to be able to respond and adapt quickly to behavioural changes.

- Set to launch in 2020, Facebook's digital currency Libra will change commerce and banking around the world as mothers embrace a new way to shop.

KEY POINTS

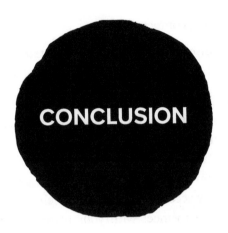

CONCLUSION

Don't miss out

I hope I've made one thing clear: if your brand continues to make the same old mistakes with mums, you will miss out on the massive potential of this market. Mothers have spoken time and again, and they are saying they are not happy with how most brands communicate with and portray them. Perhaps that includes your brand, but without the right knowledge and data you won't even know this.

For years, even decades, mothers have felt misunderstood by companies large and small. Research the world over, including my own, demonstrates that brands which fail to make a genuine effort to understand this market will not succeed. The same tired marketing messages churned out by male-dominated marketing agencies are doing more to alienate women and mums than attract them.

But this is where the opportunity lies for astute companies. Mothers are a huge yet still growing market. Brands that stick with the current methods will miss out. Brands that learn how to approach this market properly will:

- increase their sales and profits
- gain market share

- develop a strong competitive edge

- establish themselves as a reliable and trusted brand in this market, which is loyal to companies they feel understand them.

If you want to capitalise on the emerging mum trends – such as the tech-first mum, the migrant mum, the business owner mum and the solo mum – it's time to get moving. Now is the time to rethink your relationship with mothers. Brands that listen to mums, invest in understanding their needs on a regular basis, and adapt their strategy accordingly will leave their competitors behind. So I challenge you to meet with your teams, audit your current communications, identify knowledge gaps, upskill your marketing people and start investigating the relevant opportunities I have touched on in this book.

This really is the mother of all opportunities.

WORK WITH KATRINA

Katrina McCarter is the founder and CEO of Marketing to Mums, a marketing and research consultancy based in Melbourne, Australia. She is a sought-after marketing strategist who works across diverse industries helping them better understand the behaviours of mothers as shoppers, consumers and influencers. Her services include:

Board, C-Suite and Senior Management Briefings

Katrina is increasingly providing briefings to board directors, C-suite and senior managers and marketers about mums' behaviours, key trends, and strategies which are working well in the marketplace. She offers both one-off briefings as well as ongoing board advisory services to enable companies to create marketing strategies which are effective in driving growth in a competitive marketplace.

Mum Expert

In 2020 Katrina will launch her annual mum expert service where she will work with a small number of brands as their mum expert. This service provides flexibility to the client so that they can run strategy days, education sessions, review marketing strategies, test marketing creative before it hits the market, and be on hand to discuss marketing challenges in attracting mothers. This service will also provide access to Marketing to Mums new research projects, allowing brands to keep up to date with their changing behaviour and be informed about key trends before their competitors.

Marketing to Mums Assessments

The Marketing to Mums Assessment uses bespoke diagnostic tools to identify key gaps and opportunities to grow your sales and profit. It is often the first engagement a new client takes in working with Katrina and the Marketing to Mums team.

Market Research

Marketing to Mums undertakes regular research on mothers' changing behaviours every year. Their survey findings are significant and a great asset to any business that is serious about attracting more mums to their business. They are essential reading for every Board Director, CMO, Marketing Director and senior marketer.

Marketing to Mums also offers bespoke research to better understand your consumer. We engage in both qualitative and quantitative methods and can assist brands to identify their most profitable segment of the mum market. Marketing to Mums also assists brands with new product development and pre-testing of marketing creative among mothers.

Project Consulting

Marketing to Mums offers tailored and flexible project consulting for businesses who are wanting to attract more mothers and drive a commercial advantage.

All consultancy and research enquiries can be made to hello@marketingtomums.com.au

Speaker

Katrina is an award-winning international speaker who is focused on helping her audience drive sales and profit by better understanding mothers. She is a sought-after speaker for conferences and workshops across Australia and overseas. She is an engaging speaker who shares actionable recommendations based on research and a deep understanding of mothers. In October 2018 she was awarded the 'Take the Cake' Best Speaker award in New York after giving the closing keynote address at M2Moms® – The Marketing to Moms conference. In September 2018 she was the only English speaking presenter in Paris to share her research at the Moms & Marketing conference.

'I had the pleasure of programming Katrina into the content for ad:tech Sydney and I am really pleased I did. Her delivery was polished and insightful. In a world where technology is personalising everything around us, it is important that marketers think about different segments deeply and clearly, and if you are marketing to Mums, Katrina is your lady. I recommend her to anyone who needs to make meaningful connections to Mums.'

Ryf Quail, Content Director, ad:tech Sydney

'Katrina has been an excellent addition to our line up for our first ever Mums Marketing Conference, held in Sydney and Melbourne. She was pivotal in helping us launch the conference into the market by utilising her own networks for promotion and also by reaching out to a number of her own contacts personally too.

'At the event itself Katrina delivered our highest rated talk at both events; it was excellent. Katrina was voted the number 1 most engaging speaker AND number 1 most informative; we will definitely be inviting her back next year! I can't rate Katrina high enough for your event; she is the utmost professional and a genuine pleasure to work with.'

David Willey, Founder & Director, Growth Tank

'Katrina recently ran a Marketing to Mums Masterclass around the country for ProVision Eye Care, helping our member optometry practices with a practical marketing framework to better target their identified most profitable mum, based on market research Katrina coordinated. Katrina's approach was warm, highly professional, approachable and completely tailored to our audience; 200 attendees scored the Masterclass a 9.4/10! The most pleasing part? We have seen participants implement recommendations from the very next day! We will continue to work with Katrina to refine our Marketing to Mums strategies and further education for our 460+ ProVision practices.'

Sarah O'Connor, Marketing Manager, ProVision Eyecare

MARKETING TO MUMS – THE PODCAST

In November 2018, Katrina McCarter launched the world's first podcast designed to help marketing professionals and business owners improve their communications and sales to mums. It has proven a great free resource, debuting in sixth spot on the Australian Apple Podcasts Business Charts.

In Marketing to Mums – the podcast, Katrina McCarter interviews leading experts from around the globe to share latest research, insights and the subtle nuances of different mum segments. Guests include bestselling authors, international speakers, leading researchers and brand leaders who are influencing some of the biggest brands around the world. Many of these guests were also contributors to this book, *The Mother of All Opportunities*.

Marketing to Mums – the podcast caters for CMOs, Marketing Directors, Marketing Managers, Brand Managers, Digital Marketing Executives, Customer Insight teams and Business Owners.

Katrina's podcasts are approximately 30 minutes per episode, making them perfect for the commute to and from the office. They are available on all podcast platforms including Apple Podcasts, Spotify and Stitcher.